Glencoe Science

Science Inquiry Labs

Teacher Edition

 **Glencoe**

New York, New York   Columbus, Ohio   Chicago, Illinois   Peoria, Illinois   Woodland Hills, California

Glencoe Science

Glencoe

Table of Contents

To the Teacher

Science Inquiry Labs

Science Inquiry Labs is a collection of 30 hands-on activities that focus on Earth science, life science, and physical science. These labs provide excellent opportunities for enrichment, reinforcement, or independent study. You may assign or allow students to choose appropriate activities to broaden their knowledge of science concepts.

Hands-On Learning

The Teaching Strategies that begin on page TS2 provides information for introducing, developing, and concluding each activity so your classroom or laboratory is filled with students engaged in the process of discovering science.

At the middle-school level, students may have limited experience with laboratory questions and procedures. For that reason, you may wish to have them work cooperatively to accomplish each exercise. As students work on each activity, circulate to assist and answer questions about procedures.

For maximum benefit, it will be important for you and the students to discuss the lab beforehand. Students should verbalize the connection between the activity and what they already know. Use discussion as a closure activity to assess how well students have made the connections.

Safety in the Science Classroom

Whether you are a first-time or very experienced teacher, a review of safety guidelines is in order. This section deals with behaviors and actions that foster a safe learning environment. Because you serve as the role model for the behavior in the laboratory that you expect from your students, first review what you need to do to prepare for a safe classroom/laboratory. Then, on the first day of classes, introduce the safety guidelines that are the students' responsibility.

Teacher Safety Preparation

- Thoroughly review this manual and your local safety regulations. Modify any activities to comply with your local regulations. For example, open flames are NOT permitted in some states or communities.
- Be trained in first aid and CPR.
- Be aware of students with allergies or other medical conditions that might limit a their activities or require special protective equipment, such as face masks.
- Have a list of substances to be used in lab activities made available to the doctor of any pregnant teacher or student so that limitations may be determined.
- NEVER leave students unattended in the classroom.
- NEVER be alone or out of earshot of someone when you prepare lab activities or equipment.

Presenting Safety Guidelines to Students

- Review the use and location of safety equipment, evacuation guidelines, and first aid procedures. Refer to fire drill regulations and a chart of emergency procedures, which should be posted in a prominent place in the laboratory. Assign safety partners and explain their role in helping during emergencies.
- Discuss safe disposal of materials and laboratory cleanup policy.
- Preview Glencoe science activities with students and discuss the safety icons and their meanings. Point out the warning statements and the importance of heeding them. Distribute the Safety Symbols reference sheet on page ii.
- Distribute and discuss Student Laboratory and Safety Guidelines on page iii. Emphasize proper attitudes for working in the laboratory and review or present school rules regarding the consequences of misbehavior. Stress the need for safe behavior on the part of everyone involved. Review the safety guidelines and safety contract with students at least once a month.

Correlation to the Louisiana Science As Inquiry Benchmark Statements
(Grades 5–8)

The following chart illustrates how this Science Inquiry Workbook addresses Louisiana's Science As Inquiry Benchmarks.

LAB number	Life Science	Earth Science	Physical Science	Chemistry
1	X	X		
2	X			
3	X	X		X
4	X	X		
5	X		X	X
6	X	X		
7		X		
8		X	X	
9		X	X	
10	X			
11	X			X
12		X	X	
13			X	
14			X	X
15			X	
16			X	
17				X
18				X
19				X
20				X

Table of Contents

SAFETY SYMBOLS

SAFETY SYMBOLS	HAZARD	EXAMPLES	PRECAUTION	REMEDY
DISPOSAL	Special disposal procedures need to be followed.	certain chemicals, living organisms	Do not dispose of these materials in the sink or trash can.	Dispose of wastes as directed by your teacher.
BIOLOGICAL	Organisms or other biological materials that might be harmful to humans	bacteria, fungi, blood, unpreserved tissues, plant materials	Avoid skin contact with these materials. Wear mask or gloves.	Notify your teacher if you suspect contact with material. Wash hands thoroughly.
EXTREME TEMPERATURE	Objects that can burn skin by being too cold or too hot	boiling liquids, hot plates, dry ice, liquid nitrogen	Use proper protection when handling.	Go to your teacher for first aid.
SHARP OBJECT	Use of tools or glassware that can easily puncture or slice skin	razor blades, pins, scalpels, pointed tools, dissecting probes, broken glass	Practice common-sense behavior and follow guidelines for use of the tool.	Go to your teacher for first aid.
FUME	Possible danger to respiratory tract from fumes	ammonia, acetone, nail polish remover, heated sulfur, moth balls	Make sure there is good ventilation. Never smell fumes directly. Wear a mask.	Leave foul area and notify your teacher immediately.
ELECTRICAL	Possible danger from electrical shock or burn	improper grounding, liquid spills, short circuits, exposed wires	Double-check setup with teacher. Check condition of wires and apparatus.	Do not attempt to fix electrical problems. Notify your teacher immediately.
IRRITANT	Substances that can irritate the skin or mucous membranes of the respiratory tract	pollen, moth balls, steel wool, fiberglass, potassium permanganate	Wear dust mask and gloves. Practice extra care when handling these materials.	Go to your teacher for first aid.
CHEMICAL	Chemicals can react with and destroy tissue and other materials	bleaches such as hydrogen peroxide; acids such as sulfuric acid, hydrochloric acid; bases such as ammonia, sodium hydroxide	Wear goggles, gloves, and an apron.	Immediately flush the affected area with water and notify your teacher.
TOXIC	Substance may be poisonous if touched, inhaled, or swallowed.	mercury, many metal compounds, iodine, poinsettia plant parts	Follow your teacher's instructions.	Always wash hands thoroughly after use. Go to your teacher for first aid.
FLAMMABLE	Flammable chemicals may be ignited by open flame, spark, or exposed heat.	alcohol, kerosene, potassium permanganate	Avoid open flames and heat when using flammable chemicals.	Notify your teacher immediately. Use fire safety equipment if applicable.
OPEN FLAME	Open flame in use, may cause fire.	hair, clothing, paper, synthetic materials	Tie back hair and loose clothing. Follow teacher's instruction on lighting and extinguishing flames.	Notify your teacher immediately. Use fire safety equipment if applicable.

Eye Safety
Proper eye protection should be worn at all times by anyone performing or observing science activities.

Clothing Protection
This symbol appears when substances could stain or burn clothing.

Animal Safety
This symbol appears when safety of animals and students must be ensured.

Handwashing
After the lab, wash hands with soap and water before removing goggles.

Student Laboratory and Safety Guidelines

Regarding Emergencies

- Inform the teacher immediately of any mishap—glassware breakage, chemical spills, injury, fire, and so forth.
- Follow your teacher's instructions and your school's procedures in dealing with emergencies.

Regarding Your Person

- Do NOT wear clothing that is loose enough to catch on anything and avoid sandals or open-toed shoes.
- Wear protective safety gloves, goggles, and aprons as instructed.
- Do NOT wear contact lenses in the laboratory.
- Keep your hands away from your face while working in the laboratory.
- Remove synthetic fingernails before working in the lab (these are highly flammable).
- Do NOT use hair spray, mousse, or other flammable hair products just before or during laboratory work where an open flame is used (they can ignite easily).
- Tie back long hair and loose clothing to keep them away from flames and equipment.
- Remove loose jewelry—chains or bracelets—while doing lab work.
- NEVER eat or drink while in the lab or store food in lab equipment or the lab refrigerator.
- Do NOT inhale vapors or taste, touch, or smell any chemical or substance unless instructed to do so by your teacher.

Regarding Your Work

- Read all instructions before you begin a laboratory activity. Ask questions if you do not understand any part of the activity.
- Work ONLY on activities assigned by your teacher.
- Do NOT substitute other chemicals/substances for those listed in your activity.
- Do NOT begin any activity until directed to do so by your teacher.
- Do NOT handle any equipment without specific permission.
- Remain in your own work area unless given permission by your teacher to leave it.
- Do NOT point heated containers—test tubes, flasks, and so forth—at yourself or anyone else.
- Do NOT take any materials or chemicals out of the classroom.
- Stay out of storage areas unless you are instructed to be there and are supervised by your teacher.
- NEVER work alone in the laboratory.
- When using cutting equipment, always cut away from yourself and others.
- Handle living organisms or preserved specimens only when authorized by your teacher.
- Always wear heavy gloves when handling animals. If you are bitten, notify your teacher immediately.

Regarding Cleanup

- Keep work and lab areas clean, limiting the amount of easily ignitable materials.
- Turn off all burners and other equipment before leaving the lab.
- Carefully dispose of waste materials as instructed by your teacher.
- Wash your hands thoroughly with soap and warm water after each activity.

SI Reference Sheet

The International System of Units (SI) is accepted as the standard for measurement throughout most of the world. Sometimes quantities are measured using different SI units. In order to use them together in an equation, you must convert all of the quantities into the same unit. To convert, you multiply by a conversion factor. A conversion factor is a ratio that is equal to one. Make a conversion factor by building a ratio of equivalent units. Place the new units in the numerator and the old units in the denominator. For example, to convert 1.255 L to mL, multiply 1.255 L by the appropriate ratio as follows:

$$1.255 \text{ L} \times 1{,}000 \text{ mL}/1 \text{ L} = 1{,}255 \text{ mL}$$

In this equation, the unit L cancels just as if it were a number.

Frequently used SI units are listed in **Table 1.**

Table 1

Frequently Used SI Units	
Length	1 millimeter (mm) = 100 micrometers (μm) 1 centimeter (cm) = 10 millimeters (mm) 1 meter (m) = 100 centimeters (cm) 1 kilometer (km) = 1,000 meters (m) 1 light-year = 9,460,000,000,000 kilometers (km)
Area	1 square meter (m^2) = 10,000 square centimeters (cm^2) 1 square kilometer (km^2) = 1,000,000 square meters (m^2)
Volume	1 milliliter (mL) = 1 cubic centimeter (cm^3) 1 liter (L) = 1,000 milliliters (mL)
Mass	1 gram (g) = 1,000 milligrams (mg) 1 kilogram (kg) = 1,000 grams (g) 1 metric ton = 1,000 kilograms (kg)
Time	1 s = 1 second

Several other supplementary SI units are listed in **Table 2.**

Table 2

Supplementary SI Units			
Measurement	**Unit**	**Symbol**	**Expressed in base units**
Energy	joule	J	$kg \cdot m^2/s^2$
Force	newton	N	$kg \cdot m/s^2$
Power	watt	W	$kg \cdot m^2/s^3$ or J/s
Pressure	pascal	Pa	$kg/m \cdot s^2$ or $N \cdot m$

Temperature measurements in SI often are made in degrees Celsius. Celsius temperature is a supplementary unit derived from the base unit kelvin. The Celsius scale (°C) has 100 equal graduations between the freezing temperature (0°C) and the boiling temperature of water (100°C). The following relationship exists between the Celsius and kelvin temperature scales:

$$K = °C + 273$$

Figure 1

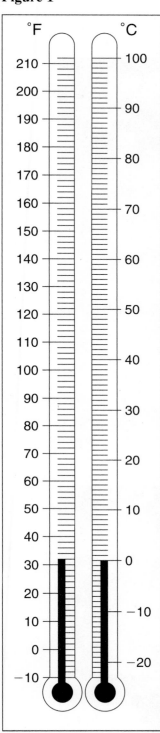

To convert from °F to °C, you can:

1. For exact amounts, use the equation at the bottom of **Table 3**

OR

2. For approximate amounts, find °F on the thermometer at the left of **Figure 1** and determine °C on the thermometer at the right.

Table 3

SI Metric to English Conversions			
	When you want to convert:	**Multiply by:**	**To find:**
Length	inches	2.54	centimeters
	centimeters	0.39	inches
	feet	0.30	meters
	meters	3.28	feet
	yards	0.91	meters
	meters	1.09	yards
	miles	1.61	kilometers
	kilometers	0.62	miles
Mass and weight*	ounces	28.35	grams
	grams	0.04	ounces
	pounds	0.45	kilograms
	kilograms	2.20	pounds
	tons	0.91	metric tons
	metric tons	1.10	tons
	pounds	4.45	newtons
	newtons	0.23	pounds
Volume	cubic inches	16.39	cubic centimeters
	milliliters	0.06	cubic inches
	cubic feet	0.03	cubic meters
	cubic meters	35.31	cubic feet
	liters	1.06	quarts
	liters	0.26	gallons
	gallons	3.78	liters
Area	square inches	6.45	square centimeters
	square centimeters	0.16	square inches
	square feet	0.09	square meters
	square meters	10.76	square feet
	square miles	2.59	square kilometers
	square kilometers	0.39	square miles
	hectares	2.47	acres
	acres	0.40	hectares
Temperature	Fahrenheit	$\frac{5}{9}(°F - 32)$	Celsius
	Celsius	$\frac{9}{5}°C + 32$	Fahrenheit

* Weight as measured in standard Earth gravity

Laboratory Equipment

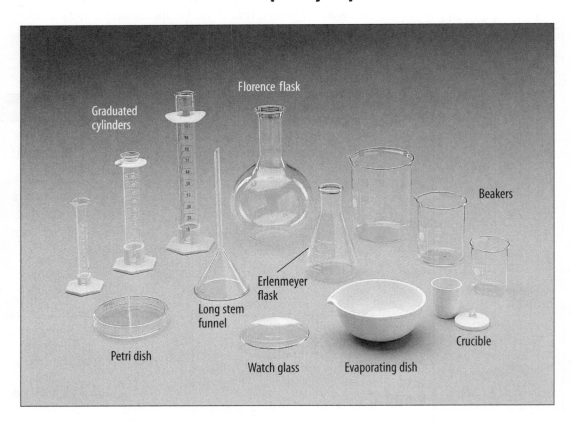

Graduated cylinders

Florence flask

Beakers

Long stem funnel

Erlenmeyer flask

Petri dish

Watch glass

Evaporating dish

Crucible

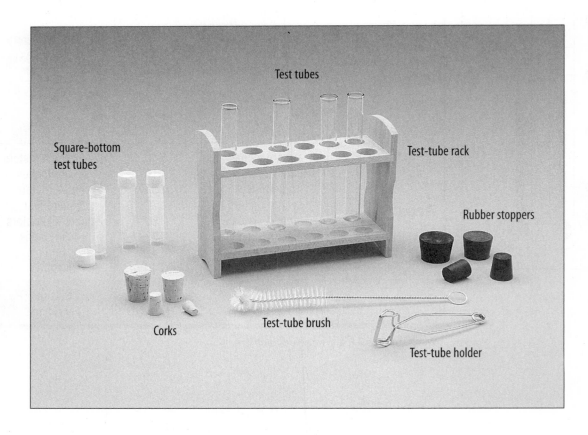

Test tubes

Square-bottom test tubes

Test-tube rack

Rubber stoppers

Corks

Test-tube brush

Test-tube holder

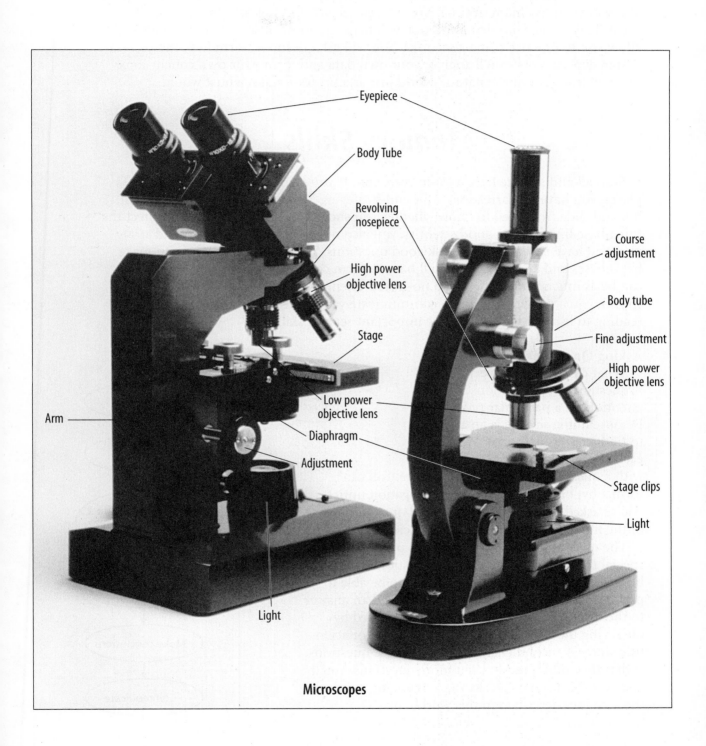

Microscopes

Science as Inquiry

Scientists learn about the natural world in many ways. As a young scientist, you also will want use many approaches to learn science and to learn how science is done. This science inquiry workbook will help you to learn science skills. It also will allow you to practice being a scientist. You will ask questions, form hypotheses, and design experiments. You'll analyze your own data and form your own conclusions. You will learn about the natural world just as a professional scientist would.

Inquiry Skills

Softball and science have a lot in common. If you want to be a good softball player, you have to learn some skills and strategies. You have to learn how to pitch, hit, and slide. You need to know whether you should cover home plate or protect the third-base line. To be a good scientist, you also need to learn some skills and strategies. You have to learn how to ask good questions. You need to know how to make hypotheses and analyze data. You'll have to form conclusions. Forming conclusions can be as much fun as pitching a no-hitter. Then, in the bottom of the ninth (so to speak), you'll need to be able to communicate your conclusions to others. Continue reading to learn more about these important science skills.

Asking Questions

What comes before every answer? A question does. Questions focus attention on a particular problem. Because doing science is an attempt to find answers and solve problems, each scientific procedure must begin with a question, as shown in the figure. You can't form a hypothesis or begin an investigation until you've asked a question. Asking good questions is one of the most important things that a scientist does.

The questions that begin scientific procedures are special in some ways. First, these questions have to be testable. This means that you have to be able to perform some type of investigation to find an answer to the question. Questions that can't be tested by observing the natural world are not suited for scientific study. A second characteristic of these questions is that they often lead to even more questions. You'll discover this for yourself as you design and conduct the activities described in this workbook.

A Typical Scientific Procedure

Do library research ⇄ Ask a question

Ask a question → Form a hypothesis

Form a hypothesis → Design and conduct an investigation to test the hypothesis

Design and conduct an investigation to test the hypothesis → Analyze the results

Analyze the results → Make conclusions

Make conclusions → Communicate

Forming Hypotheses

Once you've asked a testable question, you'll probably try to answer it. When you suggest an answer to a scientific question, you are forming a hypothesis. A hypothesis is an educated guess that answers a testable question. It often is easier to form a good hypothesis after reading about the subject in the library. The next step in your scientific procedure is to test your hypothesis.

Testing Hypotheses

To test your hypothesis, you'll want to design an investigation. You'll need to consider what steps you will follow and what materials you will use. You'll also need to think about safety. When designing an investigation, make a list of all of the steps. You also will want to list all of the necessary materials and any needed safety precautions. After your lists are complete, have your teacher approve your plan.

Next, you will want to conduct your investigation. After gathering all of the materials, you follow the steps that you developed. While conducting your investigation, you'll want to carefully record data. Data can consist of numbers, or they can be descriptions of what you observe. You'll use the data later to help you form conclusions.

Analyzing Results

After an investigation is complete, there can be a lot of data. Fortunately, there are methods that can be used to help interpret and organize these data. A method that is useful for interpreting data is using math. For example, data can be calculated as percentages. The percentages then can be organized in a table. Using tables can make it easier to read and analyze data. The table below shows the percentages of different kinds of sand grains. These sand grains are from five widely separated sand bars along the Mississippi River in Louisiana. The table also shows the average composition of the sand from these five sand bars. Calculators and computers are useful for making calculations such as these.

Sand Composition in Mississippi River Bars

Sand Bar	Quartz (%)	Feldspar (%)	Rock Pieces (%)	Other (%)
1	67	22	9	2
2	74	16	9	1
3	69	20	10	1
4	69	20	9	2
5	63	20	16	1
Average	68.4	19.6	10.6	1.4

It's sometimes easier to visualize data when they are shown in a graph. Many different kinds of graphs are used to show scientific data. However, in the case of the Mississippi River sand data, a bar graph is a good choice. Bar graphs show how much of each data category is present. Each category of data is represented by a bar in the graph. The height of a bar shows the amount of that category. Try reading the bar graph shown here.

Composition of Mississippi River Sand in Louisiana

(Bar graph: y-axis labeled "Percent abundance" ranging 0 to 80; bars — Quartz ≈ 69, Feldspar ≈ 19, Rock Pieces ≈ 10, Other ≈ 1.)

Making Conclusions

After the data have been gathered, organized, and analyzed it's time to make conclusions. This often is the most enjoyable part of an investigation. Making conclusions is fun because you find out what your data mean. You might learn something about the natural world. You also might make an important discovery. Imagine what it would be like to discover something completely new.

To make conclusions, look closely at your data and graphs. Write down any observations. Look for trends in the data, and decide whether the data show any relationships. For example, look at the Mississippi River sand data and graph. You'll notice that most of the sand grains are the mineral quartz. You might also notice that the sand composition is similar in all of the sand bars. This suggests that Mississippi River sand is similar throughout the state of Louisiana. It also suggests that the sand composition doesn't change much as it is carried along by the river.

The conclusions of a scientific investigation might or might not support the original hypothesis. If the conclusions support the hypothesis, the person doing the investigation has more confidence that the hypothesis is correct. If the conclusions do not support the hypothesis, the investigator has less confidence that the hypothesis is correct. When this occurs, new questions often are asked. These new questions can lead to new hypotheses and additional investigations.

Communicating

The last step in a scientific procedure is to communicate what you've learned to others. This can be done in many ways. One way is to make a poster. The poster could include data tables and graphs. It also might include a short summary of your procedures and conclusions. A second way to communicate is to give a short speech. You might even create your own slide show using a computer.

When scientists communicate conclusions, they often write a research paper. These papers then are read by other scientists, who comment on the research. This process is called peer review. You might want to have some of your peers review your work. They might have some helpful advice.

⬤ Inquiry Activity 1 | It's A Small World

Ocean water and freshwater contain living things that are not visible to the unaided eye. These microorganisms are very important, and scientists have identified thousands of different kinds. In this activity, you will observe microorganisms in samples of water. You then will classify the organisms.

Possible Materials

- microscope
- slides and coverslips
- prepared slides of diatoms
- live specimens of mixed algae, mixed protozoa, and/or pond water

Question

How can microorganisms be classified?

Form a Hypothesis

1. Your teacher will give you slides to examine under a microscope. Your teacher also will show you how to prepare slides from different water samples.
2. Look briefly at your slides. How do you think the living things can be classified? What kinds of features will you look for?
3. In your Science Journal, make a hypothesis to answer the question above.

Safety 🔬 🧤 ✋ 🧪 🥽

Glass slides can break, and you might be cut. Be careful plugging in your microscope; make sure

that your hands are thoroughly dry before doing so. Wash your hands throughout this experiment, and after it. Follow your teacher's instructions for cleaning up.

Test Your Hypothesis

1. Develop a plan to test your hypothesis. Have your teacher approve your plan.
2. Using the chart below, draw or make a check next to at least seven organisms that you viewed under the microscope. You also may draw all of them in your Science Journal.
3. In a table like the one on the next page, carefully record your observations of these microorganisms.

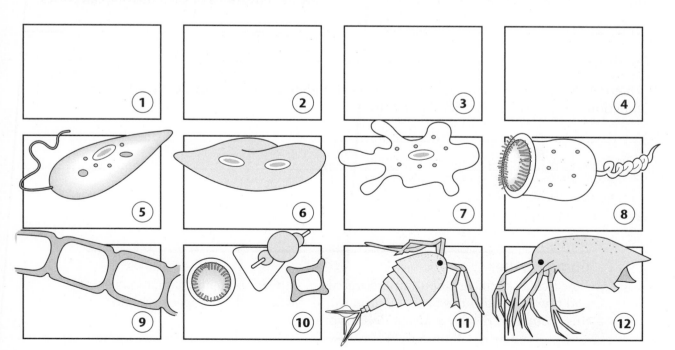

Data Table

Microorganism	Physical Appearance (shape, color, appendages)	Pattern of Movement or Means of Locomotion

Interpret Your Data

1. What patterns can you see in your data? Do some microorganisms share certain features, such as color or shape?

   _____

   _____

2. Are any of the microorganisms that you observed capable of movement? If so, how do they move?

   _____

   _____

Conclude and Apply

1. In your Science Journal, organize at least seven of the microorganisms that you observed into groups or categories. The more microorganisms you classify, the better your chances of coming up with good conclusions. Be prepared to explain the main features of each of your categories.

   _____

   _____

2. Diatoms and protozoans are among the most abundant living things in the world. What useful functions do you think they have in nature?

   _____

   _____

Going Further

Research a specific group of microorganism. Explain its main characteristics and how it contributes to the natural world. Make models of species within this group and display your models for others to see.

Inquiry Activity 2 · Designing a Classification System

What's the difference between a butterfly and an elephant? A butterfly and a moth? Being able to distinguish types of animals and plants allows scientists to organize information about them. It also allows scientists to assign each organism its own scientific name. Scientific classification is based on categories. Animals or plants in similar categories are grouped together. In this activity, you will observe pictures of 15 different animals. You then will design a classification system for the animals.

Possible Materials
- pictures of animals
- scissors
- small index cards
- tape
- glue
- pencil
- crayon

Question
How can physical characteristics be used to develop a classification system for animals?

Form a Hypothesis
Think about how characteristics can be similar or different. Suggest a hypothesis to answer the question above. Write your hypothesis in your Science Journal.

Safety
Always use caution when working with sharp objects.

Test Your Hypothesis
1. Thinking about the animal pictures provided for you, develop a plan to test your hypothesis. Feel free to change your hypothesis if necessary.
2. Make a list of the steps that you will take to design your classification system. Once you have completed your list, ask your teacher to approve your plan.
3. Begin your classification investigation. You might want to cut out the pictures of the 15 animals and attach them to index cards. You should record observations about each animal.
4. Make sure that you pay close attention to differences in physical characteristics among the animals. Important physical characteristics might include skeletal structure, skin and hair, and presence and number of limbs.

Interpret Your Data

1. Look at your list of animal observations. Do you notice any trends? For example, do all animals with 2 legs have wings? Use your data to make statements about how you grouped your animals.

_____

_____

2. On a piece of poster board, use your pictures and observations to show your classification system. Group similar animals and separate dissimilar animals. You might need to include important statements such as "Animals with four legs and hair" to make the selections clear.

Conclude and Apply

1. If an additional animal was added to your animal collection, would you be able to classify this new animal? Give an example.

_____

_____

Going Further
Choose 4–8 animals that you consider closely related to each other (example: lions, tigers, house cats, cheetahs, and leopards). Research their scientific names. How are the names similar? How are they different? Are you able to make any conclusions about which animals are most closely related?

⬤ Inquiry Activity 3 | Effects of Acid Rain

Acid rain can harm plants and animals. When acid rain falls on forests, the trees can be damaged. Acid rain also can kill fish by making lakes more acidic. In this activity, you will find out how acid rain might affect crops such as corn.

Background

Before you begin your investigation, you'll need to know about pH values. These values can tell you about the acidity of water. When the pH value of water is less than 7, the water is acidic. The lower the pH value is, the more acidic the water is. When water has a pH value that is greater than 7, the water is basic. Water with a pH value equal to 7 is neutral. You can find the pH of water using pH paper or a computer probe.

Pollution can make rainwater more acidic than it normally is. Power plants and cars give off pollutants that can combine with water in the atmosphere to form acid. Acid rain occurs when this acidic water falls to Earth.

Possible Materials

- soil
- corn seeds
- planting pots
- metric ruler
- rainwater
- vinegar
- pH paper or pH probe
- 50-mL cylinder
- plant light or window

Question

What effect does acid rain have on corn plants?

Form a Hypothesis

Think about what you already know about acid rain. Now, make a hypothesis to answer the question above. Write your hypothesis in your Science Journal.

Safety 🖐 🧪 🥽

Be careful with vinegar. It can irritate your eyes. Never touch a hot plant light. Wash your hands after working with vinegar or soil.

Test Your Hypothesis

1. Think about the materials that have been provided for you. How will you test your hypothesis?
2. Make a list of the steps that you will follow. You probably will want to grow corn in two different pots. How will you use vinegar to model acid rain? How will you use pH paper or a pH probe? Will one pot receive normal rainwater? How often will you measure the height of your corn plants? Don't forget that some factors in an experiment must be held

constant. Once you have completed your list, ask your teacher to approve your plan.
3. Carry out your investigation. Take careful notes about the height of your corn plants. You might want to use a table like the one on the next page to organize your data.

Data Table

Corn Plants	Height (mm)							
	Day 2	Day 4	Day 6	Day 8	Day 10	Day 12	Day 14	Day 16
Pot A (watered with normal rain)								
Pot B (watered with acid rain)								

Interpret Your Data

1. Make a line graph that shows how the corn plants grew through time. Label the horizontal axis *Time (days)* and the vertical axis *Height (mm)*. You should use one color to draw the line for the plant(s) that received normal rain. Then, use a different color to draw the line for the plant(s) that received acid rain. Make a legend that shows which color is for which plant(s).

2. Look at your table and your graph. What differences do you notice about how the plants in the different pots grew?

_____

_____

_____

Conclude and Apply

1. What effect could acid rain have on a farmer's corn field?

_____

_____

_____

2. Lime can increase the pH of water. Why do you think some farmers spread lime on their fields?

_____

_____

_____

Going Further
Scientists often ask other scientists to review their work. Talk to some of your classmates about your data. Work together to understand your data better than you did before.

Inquiry Activity 4 | Growth Rings as Indicators of Climate

Tree rings are used to learn what the climate of a region was like in the past. Scientists can tell whether a region was wet or dry or cold or warm. By studying past climates, scientists can better understand how Earth's climate might change in the future. In this activity, you will interpret past climatic conditions from tree rings.

Background

New wood is added to tree trunks each year. In the spring, a tree produces earlywood. The cells in earlywood are comparatively large. In the summer, much smaller cells are produced to form latewood. The boundary between one year's latewood and the next year's earlywood separates the rings of wood added to a tree trunk each year.

The number and thickness of tree rings are important information. You can find the age of a tree by counting its rings. The thickness of tree rings is related to climate. When climatic conditions are good, tree rings are thick. When climatic conditions are bad, tree rings are thin.

Possible Materials
- metric ruler

Question

How can tree rings be used to learn how much rainfall occurred in past years?

Form a Hypothesis

Form a hypothesis to answer the question above. Write your hypothesis in your Science Journal.

Safety 🥽

Test Your Hypothesis

1. Look at Figures 2, 3, and 4 on the next page. These figures are drawings of tree trunks from trees that grew in relatively mild climates. How will these drawings allow you to test your hypothesis?
2. Make a list of the steps that you will follow to determine the age of each tree represented by the drawings. Make a list of the steps that you will use to infer past rainfall amounts received by each tree. You might want to use a table like the one on the next page to organize your data. Once you have completed your lists, ask your teacher to approve your plan.

3. Carry out your investigation. Use care when making measurements. You'll want your data to be as accurate as possible.

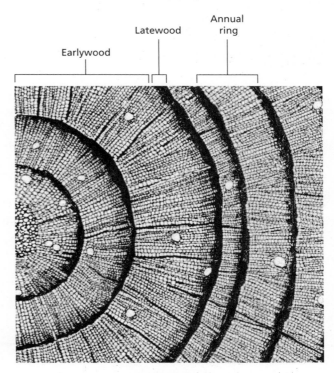

Earlywood   Latewood   Annual ring

FIGURE 1

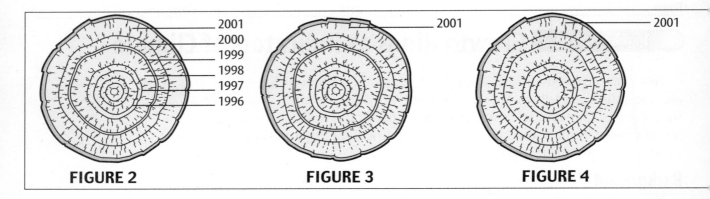

FIGURE 2   FIGURE 3   FIGURE 4

Data and Conclusions

Tree	Number of Rings	Age of Tree	Widest Ring (year)	Narrowest Ring (year)
Figure 2				
Figure 3				
Figure 4				

Interpret Your Data

1. Look at the data that you gathered about the number of rings in each tree trunk. What was the age of each tree? How do you know? Complete the *Age of Tree* column of your table.

_____

_____

Conclude and Apply

1. During which year did the tree in Figure 2 receive the most rain? The least? During which years did the trees in Figures 3 and 4 receive the most rain? The least? How do you know?

_____

_____

2. The trees represented by Figures 2, 3, and 4 grew in different locations. In which of these locations do you think conditions were most suited for growth? Why?

_____

_____

Going Further

Research to find out how scientists use a technique called crossdating to extend tree ring information back in time. Make a poster to show what you learn.

Inquiry Activity 5 # Radiation and Its Effects on Seeds

When seeds are exposed to nuclear radiation, changes occur. Seeds contain genetic material called DNA. The DNA in seeds determines the characteristics of the plants that grow from them. Radiation can change DNA. The type of seeds and the amount of radiation absorbed determine the extent of the change. In this investigation, you will observe plants grown from irradiated seeds.

Possible Materials

- containers for planting (boxes, pots, or plastic cups)
- potting soil
- seeds that have not been irradiated
- seeds that have received different doses of radiation
- graph paper
- metric ruler
- water
- plant light or window

Question

How are plants grown from irradiated seeds different from plants grown from normal seeds?

Form a Hypothesis

Think about what you already know about radiation. Suggest a hypothesis to the question above. Write your hypothesis in your Science Journal.

Safety

Keep potting soil away from your face. It can irritate your eyes.

Test Your Hypothesis

1. Think about the materials that have been provided for you. How will you test your hypothesis?
2. Make a list of the steps that you will follow. You probably will want to grow seeds exposed to different amounts of radiation in different pots. What labels will you use? Will all seeds have the same amount of soil, water and sunlight? How often will you observe the seedlings? Height is just one way to measure plant growth. What other features might you observe to notice the effects of radiation? Once you have completed your list, ask your teacher to approve your plan.
3. Carry out your investigation. Take careful notes about your observations. You might find that making a table in which to record your descriptions is a good way to manage data.
4. Make certain that you pay close attention to differences among the plants grown from different seeds. Important things to notice include sprouting and growth rates; differences in size, color, and shape; and number and location of stems and leaves.

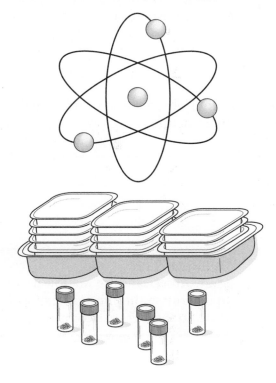

Data Table

Container Number	Amount of Radiation	Observations					
		Day ___	Day ___	Day ___	Day ___	Day ___	Day ___

Interpret Your Data

1. Using graph paper, make a line graph that shows the height of the plants in each pot through time. Label the horizontal axis *Time (days)* and the vertical axis *Height (mm)*. You should use one color to draw the line for the plants that grew from the seeds that received no radiation. Then, use different colors to draw lines for the plants that grew from seeds that received varying amounts of radiation. Make a legend that shows which color represents which plants. Be sure to give your graph a title.

2. Look at your table and your graph. Compare and contrast the growth rates of the plants grown from the different types of seed. Describe your observations.

_____

_____

Conclude and Apply

1. Which characteristics of your seedlings seemed to be most affected by the radiation? Which characteristics were least affected?

_____

_____

2. Based on your observations of irradiated plant growth, what differences would you expect to find in the root structure and growth of these same plants? How could you test your expectation?

_____

_____

Going Further
Many Americans use microwave ovens in their homes. Design an experiment to determine the effects of exposing seeds to different amounts of microwaves. How do these results compare with the results that you obtained earlier?

Inquiry Activity 6 # Survival in Extreme Climates

In this activity, you will learn how cactus plants are able to survive in desert climates.

Background

Desert plants and animals are adapted to an extreme environment. The daily change of air temperature can be more than 30°C. Summer high temperatures can be 50°C, and winter low temperatures can be less than 0°C. Deserts are also the driest environments on Earth. They often get less than 25 cm of rainfall in a year.

Possible Materials

- plastic covering or newspaper
- 3–5 different types of house plants, such as ferns or flowering plants; and at least one type of small cactus plant
- medium-size bowl
- toothpicks
- craft stick
- small paintbrush
- ruler

Question

What characteristics of cactus plants make them better suited than other plants to survive in desert conditions?

Form a Hypothesis

Think about specific differences between the cactus plants and the other plants you have been given. How are they shaped? How are the leaves different? In your Science Journal, write a hypothesis to answer to the question above.

Safety

Needles on the cactus plants can puncture and irritate your skin. Use gloves and, whenever possible, a toothpick or craft stick when examining a cactus.

Test Your Hypothesis

1. Make a list of specific procedures that you will use to test your hypothesis. Don't limit your investigation. You may examine any part of the plants, even the roots, to test your hypothesis.
2. In your Science Journal, you might want to make a table like the one on the next page to organize your observations.

Data Table

Plant Type	Stem	Leaves	Roots
1.			
2.			
3.			
4.			
5.			
6.			
7.			

Interpret Your Data

1. How do cactus plant structures differ from those of the other plants?

_____

_____

_____

_____

Conclude and Apply

1. Think about the advantages that cactus plant structures might offer in a desert environment. What do your observations tell you about how cactus plants are adapted to survive in the desert?

_____

_____

_____

_____

Going Further
Research another unusual type of environment, such as a rain forest or inland mountain range. Find out what types of plants inhabit that environment and explain how they are adapted to survive there. Compare your conclusions with those of your classmates.

Inquiry Activity 7 **Upfolds and Downfolds**

The movement of Earth's plates can cause rock layers to fold. This often occurs when two plates collide to form mountains. Through time, erosion can lower the mountains and expose the folded rock. In this activity, you'll learn how rock layers are arranged in folds.

Background

You might remember the principle of superposition. It states that the oldest rock layer in a stack of rock layers is at the bottom. However, the principle of superposition might not apply to rock layers that have been folded or faulted.

Rock layers can be folded in two basic ways. The layers can be folded down, or the layers can be folded up. Downfolds are called synclines. Upfolds are called anticlines. In some mountain regions, the rock layers have been folded into alternating anticlines and synclines.

Possible Materials
■ modeling clay (4 colors)
■ plastic knife
■ paper
■ colored pencils

Question

Where are the oldest rock layers in anticlines and synclines that are exposed at Earth's surface?

Form a Hypothesis

Form a hypothesis to answer the question above. You might find that drawing sketches is helpful.

Safety 🧤 🧼 🥽

Be careful with plastic knives. Wash your hands after making your models.

Test Your Hypothesis

1. Think about the materials that have been provided for you. How will you test your hypothesis?
2. Make a list of the steps that you will follow. You'll probably want to make two flat stacks, each having four different-colored layers of clay. How will you know which colors represent older rock layers and which represent younger rock layers? You might want to write the order from oldest to youngest in the table on the next page.
3. How will you form an anticline and a syncline? How will you use the plastic knife to model erosion of the folds? Once you have

completed your list, ask your teacher to approve your plan.

4. Carry out your investigation. Make sketches of what you observe.

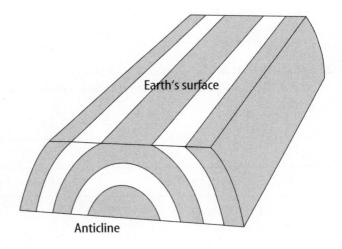

Earth's surface

Anticline

Layer Color	Stack for Anticline	Stack for Syncline
Color of youngest rock layer		
Color of next-to-youngest rock layer		
Color of next-to-oldest rock layer		
Color of oldest rock layer		

Interpret Your Data

1. Look at the tops and sides of the anticline and syncline models that you made. How are the rock layers arranged?

_____

_____

_____

Conclude and Apply

1. In your own words, describe an anticline and a syncline. Where is the oldest rock layer at Earth's surface in each case?

_____

_____

_____

2. Imagine that a friend gave you a map that showed folded rock layers at Earth's surface. If you knew the ages of the rock layers, how could you identify whether a fold was an anticline or a syncline?

_____

_____

_____

Going Further
Research to learn about the relationship between anticlines and oil. Create a poster to illustrate what you discover. Why do think it is important for scientists to be able to recognize anticlines?

Inquiry Activity 8   Making Waves

Beaches are affected by the waves that come ashore. However, all beaches are not affected in the same way. Waves cause beaches with coarse sand to have different slopes than beaches with fine sand. In this activity, you will learn about the relationship between sand grain size and beach slope.

Possible Materials

- wave tank or plastic tub (1 m × 0.5 m × 15 cm) (2)
- coarse sand (dry)
- fine sand (dry)
- wooden board (about 30 cm long)
- water
- clock or watch
- grease pencil
- protractor
- metric ruler
- pitcher
- sandbox shovel

Question

How does the size of beach sand grains affect the slope of the beach?

Form a Hypothesis

Think about beaches that you have seen. Now, make a hypothesis to answer the question above. Write your hypothesis in your Science Journal.

Safety

Do not use water near any type of electrical appliance. Do not put sand in the sink. It might plug the drain. Your teacher will tell you how to dispose of used sand.

Test Your Hypothesis

1. Think about the materials that have been provided for you. How will you test your hypothesis?
2. Make a list of the steps that you will follow. You probably will want to put coarse sand in one tub and fine sand in the other. How will you model a beach? How will you model waves? How long will you produce waves? What will you use to measure the slope of the beaches? Don't forget that some factors must be held constant in an experiment. Once you have completed your list, ask your teacher to approve your plan.
3. Carry out your experiment. Make careful measurements of beach slope. You might want to make a table in which to record your data.

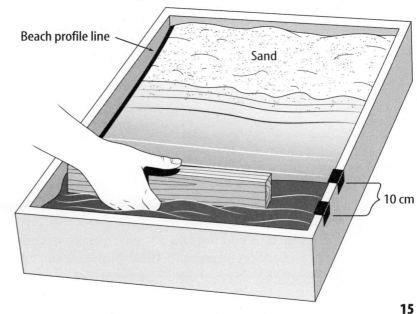

Beach profile line

Sand

10 cm

Interpret Your Data

1. Look carefully at the data that you obtained. Which beach (coarse or fine) had the higher slope angle? Which had the lower angle? How much is the difference?

_____

_____

_____

2. Use your metric ruler and a calculator to find the average size of the fine sand grains and the average size of the coarse sand grains. To do this, you should measure ten grains of each type of sand. Then, average the sizes of the ten fine sand grains. Also average the sizes of the ten coarse sand grains. Record your data.

	Grain Measurements (mm)										Average (mm)
	1	2	3	4	5	6	7	8	9	10	
Fine											
Coarse											

3. Make a graph showing the relationship between beach slope and grain size. Label the x-axis of your graph *Grain size (mm)*. Label the y-axis *Beach slope (degrees)*. Use the average grain sizes and the beach slope angles that you measured to complete your graph. Plot the point for fine sand. Plot the point for coarse sand. Connect these points with a straight line.

Conclude and Apply

1. How does the slope of a beach vary with grain size? (Hint: the graph that you made should help you answer this question.)

_____

_____

_____

2. If a friend gave you a sample of sand from an unknown beach, how could you predict the approximate slope of that beach?

_____

_____

_____

Going Further

Do research to find out why the government has paid for studies of beaches. Why are beaches important? What problems can occur on beach-front property?

● Inquiry Activity 9 | A Trip Around the World

Because Earth rotates from west to east, points on Earth's surface are in constant motion. This west to east motion is called linear motion. Speed is the rate at which motion occurs. Speed is calculated using the following formula: speed = distance ÷ time. In this investigation, you will discover how linear speed varies with Earth's latitude.

Background

Latitude is used to measure position north or south of Earth's equator. The equator has a latitude of 0°. The north pole has a latitude of 90° north, because it is 90° away from the equator toward the north. The south pole is 90° south latitude. Places in between the poles and the equator have latitudes that are in between 0° and 90°, north or south.

Longitude is used to measure position east or west of the prime meridian. The prime meridian is an imaginary line on Earth's surface that connects Earth's poles and runs through Greenwich, England. The prime meridian has a longitude of 0°. Other places have longitude values that are between 0° and 180°, either east or west of the prime meridian.

Possible Materials

- a globe that is mounted on an axis
- masking tape
- stopwatch
- string
- meterstick
- calculator

Question

How does linear speed vary with latitude?

Form a Hypothesis

Look at your globe and think about the meaning of linear speed. Now, make a hypothesis to answer the question above. Write your hypothesis in your Science Journal.

Safety 🥽

Test Your Hypothesis

1. Think about the materials that have been provided for you. How will you test your hypothesis?
2. Make a list of the steps that you will follow. You probably will want to find the linear speed at the equator, 30°N latitude, 60°N latitude, and the north pole. How will you determine distance? How will you measure time? How will you use the string and the tape? Once you have completed your list, ask your teacher to approve your plan.
3. Carry out your investigation. You might want to record your data in tables like those on the next page.

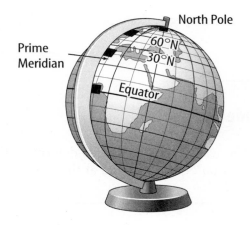

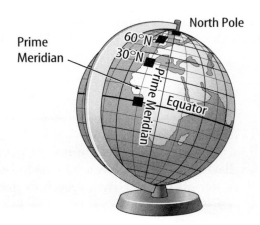

Table 1

Latitude	Distance Moved (cm)		
	1 second	2 seconds	3 seconds
Equator			
30°N			
60°N			
North pole			

Table 2

Latitude	Linear Speed (cm/s)		
	Trial 1	Trial 2	Trial 3
Equator			
30°N			
60°N			
North pole			

Interpret Your Data

1. Look at the speeds that you calculated. How does linear speed vary with latitude?

_____

_____

Conclude and Apply

1. Use the scale on your globe to determine the true distance around Earth at the equator, 30°N latitude, 60°N latitude, and at the north pole. Record these distances.

_____

_____

2. Earth rotates once in about 24 hours. Using the distances that you determined in question 1, calculate the actual linear speeds for Earth at each latitude. Show your work.

Going Further

Do research to learn about the Coriolis effect. How did an understanding of Earth's rotation allow scientists to better understand the flow of air and ocean water on Earth? Give a speech to the class explaining what you learn.

Inquiry Activity 10 Investigating Diatomite

Fossils occur in many sizes. You're familiar with large fossils such as dinosaur bones. You also might have seen fossils of trilobites, snails, or leaves. But many fossils, called microfossils, are too small to be seen with the unaided eye. In this activity, you will observe a common type of microfossil.

Background

Some microscopic organisms produce shells. These organisms are common in oceans and lakes. Some float near the surface, and others live at greater depths. When these organisms die, their shells accumulate on the bottom to form sediment.

Diatomite is a kind of sedimentary rock. It forms from sediment that consists of the shells of a particular type of algae. The algae are called diatoms, and their shells are made from silica. Diatom-shell sediment occurs at many places on the ocean floor today. It also occurs on some lake bottoms.

Possible Materials

- stereomicroscope
- microscope lamp
- diatomite
- fine artist's paintbrush
- square of black construction paper
- small laboratory spatula

Question

What does diatomite look like under a microscope?

Form a Hypothesis

Form a hypothesis to answer the question above. Write your hypothesis in your Science Journal.

Safety

Do not inhale or swallow diatomite. Don't rub your eyes with diatomite-soiled hands. Wash your hands after the activity. Your teacher will tell you how to dispose of your sample.

Test Your Hypothesis

1. Think about the materials that have been provided for you. How will you test your hypothesis?
2. Make a list of the steps that you will follow. How will you observe your sample? What procedures will you follow? After you have completed your list, have your teacher approve your plan.
3. Carry out your investigation. Take careful notes about what you observe through the microscope. You might want to draw some sketches of what you see.

Diatom shell

Sketch Your Fossils Here

Interpret Your Data

1. Write descriptions of the different microfossils that you observed on the lines below.

_____

_____

_____

_____

_____

_____

Conclude and Apply

1. In your own words, explain how diatomite forms.

_____

_____

_____

2. What do you think scientists learn by studying microfossils?

_____

_____

_____

Going Further
Research other types of microfossils. What types of sediments do they produce? What types of rocks can these sediments form? Communicate what you learn by making and displaying a poster.

Inquiry Activity 11   Coal: What's My Rank?

Although some people joke about getting a lump of coal as a gift, coal is a valuable rock. Much of this country's electricity is generated by burning coal. The coal formed from plants that lived in ancient swamps. Through millions of years and under the influence of heat and pressure, the plant matter gradually changed into rock. In this activity, you will learn about the properties of coal. You also will learn about how coal is classified according to its rank.

> ## Possible Materials
> - anthracite coal
> - bituminous coal
> - subbituminous coal (optional)
> - lignite coal
> - hand lens
> - penny

Question

What are the physical properties of the different types of coal? What changes occur through time as coal is subjected to more heat and pressure?

Form a Hypothesis

Based on your research or what you already know about coal, suggest a hypothesis, or possible answer, to the questions above. Write your hypothesis in your Science Journal.

Safety

Don't hit rocks against the table. You can see how coal breaks by looking at the already broken edges. Wash your hands after the activity.

Test Your Hypothesis

1. Considering the rock samples and equipment that are provided for you, develop a plan to test your hypothesis. Feel free to change your hypothesis if necessary.
2. Make a list of the steps that you will take during this investigation. Once you have completed the list, ask your teacher to approve your plan.
3. Carry out your investigation as planned. Take careful notes about your observations as you work. You might find that making a table in which to record descriptions of the different types of coal is a good way to manage data.

4. Make certain that you pay close attention to differences in physical properties among the different samples. Important physical properties are hardness and the way the rocks break.

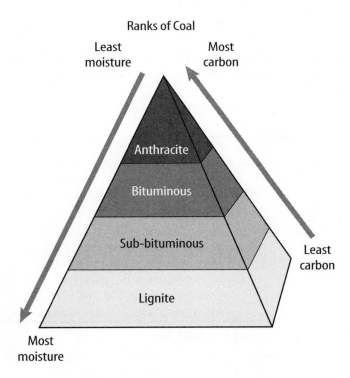

Ranks of Coal

Interpret Your Data

1. Look at the data that you acquired about the different types of coal. Do you notice any trends? For example, are some samples of coal harder than other samples or do some samples break in a different way than others do?

_____

_____

_____

2. Coal changes as it is subjected to increasing amounts of heat and pressure within Earth. The rank of coal depends upon the highest amount of heat and pressure to which it was exposed. Anthracite coal was subjected to the most heat and pressure, and lignite coal was subjected to the least. Using the figure on the previous page, identify the rank of each of your coal samples.

_____

_____

_____

Conclude and Apply

1. What properties of coal change as the coal is exposed to more heat and pressure within Earth? Describe the changes that occur.

_____

_____

_____

2. Predict what will happen to a layer of lignite coal as it is buried under more sediment and rock and then finally undergoes metamorphism at high temperature and pressure.

_____

_____

_____

Going Further

Make a poster showing how plants in a swamp might become anthracite coal after millions of years. Display your poster for others to see.

Inquiry Activity 12 | Tornado in a Jar

A tornado is a violently rotating column of air that extends from a cloud to the ground. Most tornadoes form because of wind shear in a cloud. Wind shear means that air is moving in different directions at different heights. Wind shear can cause air in a cloud to spin around in circles. If this spinning air gets tilted down toward the ground, a tornado might occur. In this activity, you will model a tornado.

Possible Materials
- 1-quart plastic or glass jar with lid
- water
- 10 mL of liquid dish soap
- 10 mL of vinegar
- a few drops of food coloring

Question
How does the air move in a tornado?

Form a Hypothesis
Form a hypothesis to answer the question above. Write your hypothesis in your Science Journal.

Safety 🧤 🥽
Be careful with vinegar and dish soap. They can irritate your eyes. Wash your hands after using them.

Test Your Hypothesis
1. Think about the materials that have been provided for you. How will you test your hypothesis?
2. Make a list of the steps that you will follow. You'll probably want to put the dish soap, vinegar, and food coloring in the jar with water. How will you model a tornado? How will you keep the water from spilling? Once you have completed your list, ask your teacher to approve your plan.
3. Carry out your investigation. Take careful notes about what you observe.

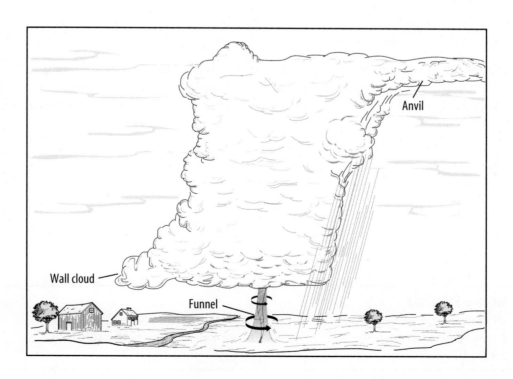

Anvil

Wall cloud

Funnel

Interpret Your Data

1. Describe and sketch what you observed during your experiment.

_____

_____

_____

_____

Drawing:

Conclude and Apply

1. How was the model that you made similar to a tornado? How was it different?

_____

_____

_____

_____

2. During the formation of a tornado, a column of rotating air becomes narrower and a funnel reaches down to the ground. Thinking about what happens when a spinning ice skater pulls her arms close to her body, describe what you think happens to the column of air when it becomes narrower.

_____

_____

_____

Going Further
Research to find out what scientists are doing to better understand how tornadoes develop. Why is this research important? How is the research being funded?

Inquiry Activity 13 | Identifying Metals and Nonmetals

An electric current can flow through a metal. An electric current will not flow through a nonmetal. In this activity, you will make a conductivity tester. Then you will test samples with it.

Background

Metals are good conductors of electricity because they have low resistance. Electrons flow freely in them. Nonmetals are not good conductors because they have high resistance to the movement of electrons. A metal sample can complete an electric circuit and cause a lightbulb to light. A nonmetal sample can not.

Possible Materials

- 1.5-V dry cell
- 1.5-V lightbulb
- insulated wires (3)
- tape
- battery holder (optional)
- bulb socket (optional)
- zinc strip
- glass rod
- copper strip
- rubber sample
- wood sample
- iron sample
- unknown sample

Question

How can you determine whether an unknown is a metal or a nonmetal?

Form a Hypothesis

Based on the background, form a hypothesis to answer the question above. Write your hypothesis in your Science Journal.

Safety

Test Your Hypothesis

1. Think about the materials that have been provided for you. Design an electrical circuit in which the bulb will light if the sample conducts electricity and will not light if the sample does not conduct electricity. When you have completed your setup, ask your teacher to approve it. Then sketch it in your Science Journal.

2. Carefully test each sample. Enter your data in a table like the one on the next page.

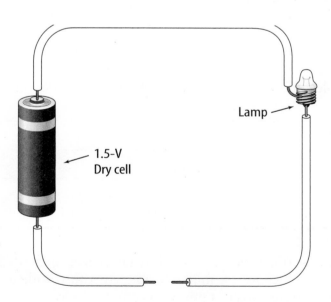

Lamp

1.5-V
Dry cell

Sample Tested	Did the bulb light?	Does it conduct electricity?	Is it a metal or a nonmetal?	Other Observations

Interpret Your Data

1. Which samples are metals? How do you know?

_____

_____

_____

2. Which samples are nonmetals? How do you know?

_____

_____

_____

3. What physical properties do all of the metals have in common?

_____

_____

_____

Conclude and Apply

1. Is your unknown sample a metal or a nonmetal? What is your evidence?

_____

_____

_____

Going Further
Explain why the electrical conductivity of metals makes them useful. Then list some situations in which metals might be unsafe because of their ability to conduct electric current. Create a poster to communicate what you learn.

Inquiry Activity 14 # The Inside Story of Packaging

In this activity, you will investigate why different types of plastic packages are used for different products.

Background

When you buy an item at a supermarket, you purchase two things—the item and its package. The package allows you to carry and store the product. A good package also protects its contents from damage, contamination, or spoilage. The properties of a package must be well suited to the properties of the product that it contains.

Many packages are made from plastics. To aid in recycling, the packaging industry uses a code to indicate the main component of a plastic container. This code is found on the bottom of a package, inside a triangle of arrows. It is a number between 1 and 6. The code allows plastic to be sorted for recycling.

Possible Materials

- at least ten different plastic packages (These should include a wide variety of packages, such as ones for food, detergents, shampoo, and other consumer goods.)

Question

Why and how do the properties of plastic packages differ from one product to another?

Form a Hypothesis

Think about the products that your packages would contain. What qualities would the packages need to have? Then, in your Science Journal, write a hypothesis to answer the question above.

Safety

Do not open any of the packages. Your teacher will make sure that the outside of each package has been washed. It is still a good idea to wash your hands after handling the packages.

Test Your Hypothesis

1. Write out a plan for examining and categorizing your packages. What qualities will you look for to test your hypothesis?
2. Make a table in your Science Journal to organize your observations. The table on the next page shows one possible strategy.

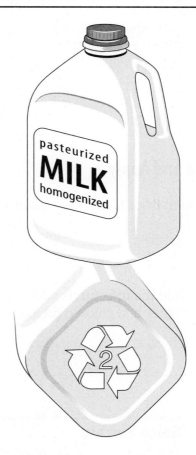

Data Table

Package Code	Product	Physical Properties

Interpret Your Data

1. What properties do the products in containers marked with the same codes share?

_____

_____

2. How do containers with different codes compare? How were some same-coded containers different from each other?

_____

_____

_____

Conclude and Apply

1. What kind of product is a container coded "1" suited for? A container coded "2"?

_____

_____

2. Why would manufacturers add colored pigment to the plastic used in some containers? When wouldn't they add colored pigment?

_____

_____

Going Further

Do research to determine what types of materials are made from recycled plastic with different codes. List several ways plastic has aided the packaging industry, and how recycling of plastic has benefited our society.

⬤ Inquiry Activity 15   Lenses that Magnify

You probably have used a magnifying glass to make objects appear larger. A magnifying glass is a convex lens. Parallel light rays passing through a convex lens are bent toward a single point called the focal point. The distance between the center of the lens and the focal point is called the focal length. In this activity you will discover the relationship between the curvature of a lens and its focal length.

Possible Materials

- masking tape
- white index card
- flashlight
- convex lenses with different curvature (3)
- metric ruler

Question

How are lens curvature and focal length related?

Form a Hypothesis

Form a hypothesis to answer the question above. Write your hypothesis in your Science Journal.

Safety

Do not focus the light from a lens at other people because it can damage eyes. Do not focus sunlight on objects because it can start a fire.

Test Your Hypothesis

1. Think about the materials that have been provided for you and study the figure on this page. What will you measure to determine focal length? Light from a flash-light several meters away from the lens is close enough to parallel to find the focal length. The light is focused when the spot on the screen is as small as possible.
2. Make a list of the steps that you will follow. Once you have completed your list, ask your teacher to approve your plan.
3. Carry out your experiment. You might want to record your data in a table like the one on the next page.

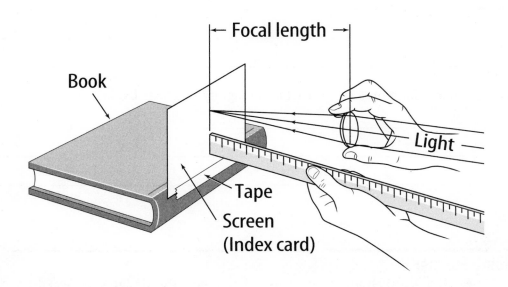

Book — Focal length — Light — Tape — Screen (Index card)

Data Table

Curvature of Lens	Focal Length (cm)
Least curvature	
Intermediate curvature	
Most curvature	

Interpret Your Data

1. Look at the data that you acquired. How is the curvature of a lens related to its focal length?

   _____

   _____

   _____

2. Select the lens with the least curvature and the lens with the most curvature. Use these two lenses to look at the print on this page. Which lens has the higher magnification? How is the curvature of a lens related to its magnification?

   _____

   _____

   _____

Conclude and Apply

1. You are given two lenses. One lens has a focal length of 5 cm. The other has a focal length of 10 cm. Which lens has the greater curvature?

   _____

   _____

   _____

2. Can a drop of water resting on a surface act as a magnifying glass? Explain.

   _____

   _____

   _____

Going Further

Do research to learn about Fresnel lenses. Learn how this design saves weight (and material) compared to other lenses. Maybe you can find a "flat" magnifier.

Inquiry Activity 16   Electrolytes and Conductivity

Introduction

In this activity, you will create an electric current in salt water. This will be part of a circuit that includes a flashlight bulb. Commercially, an electric current in a liquid is used to refine aluminum.

Background

Materials that carry an electric current are called conductors. Pure water is not a conductor. Tap water and sports drinks are conductors. Salt water is a better conductor. A solution that conducts an electric current is called an electrolyte.

Possible Materials

- metric ruler
- 2 pieces of household aluminum foil (about 30 cm × 14 cm)
- pencil
- 250-mL beaker
- water
- 5 g table salt (sodium chloride)
- stirring rod
- flashlight batteries (2)
- battery holders (optional) (2)
- flashlight bulb
- alligator clips (4)
- wire (about 15 cm long) (4)

Question

How does electrode size affect conductivity?

Form a Hypothesis

Form a hypothesis to answer the question above. Write your hypothesis in your Science Journal.

Safety

Use care when handling alligator clips and wires.

Test Your Hypothesis

1. Think about the materials that have been provided for you. Design an electrical circuit that includes the beaker of salt water. One setup is shown in the drawing. You will complete the circuit by touching the base of the flashlight bulb to the dry end of the marked electrode. The electrodes are made by folding each piece of aluminum foil into a 30 cm × 2 cm strip. When you have completed your setup, ask your teacher to approve it. Then sketch it in your Science Journal.

2. In the setup shown below, you can test your electrical connections by briefly touching the base of the flashlight bulb to the dry part of the unmarked electrode. What would you expect to see? Test your electrical connections.

3. Plan what data to take to test your hypothesis. Carry out your experiment and record your observations in your Science Journal.

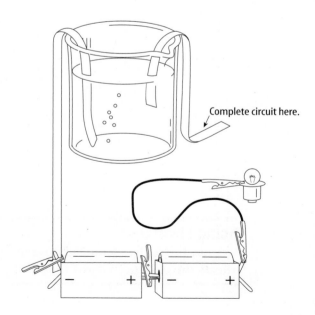

Complete circuit here.

Interpret Your Data

1. Look carefully at your data. Which electrode length produced the brightest light?

_____

_____

_____

_____

Conclude and Apply

1. How did you know that there was a closed circuit?

_____

_____

_____

_____

2. What happened to the conductivity of the solution as the amount of submerged electrode increased?

_____

_____

_____

_____

3. Which data inform you about the conductivity?

_____

_____

_____

_____

Going Further
Do you think the distance between two electrodes in a conducting solution affects the conductivity of the solution? Form a hypothesis and test it.

Inquiry Activity 17 Curds and Whey

The pH scale is a measure of how acidic or basic a substance is. The pH value can determine whether a chemical reaction will occur. For example, the pH of milk determines whether curds will form, as in the production of cottage cheese. In this activity, you will observe what happens when different substances are added to milk.

Background

The pH of a substance can be measured with pH paper. This method can determine whether a solution is acidic or basic. Acids have a pH of less than 7, and bases have a pH of more than 7. Pure water is neutral and has a pH of 7. Milk curdles when the pH approaches 4.6. The remaining liquid is called whey.

Possible Materials

- pH paper
- vinegar
- lemon juice
- tea
- diluted chocolate syrup
- milk
- graduated cylinder
- plastic cups (4)
- stirring rod

Question

Which of the following substances will cause milk to curdle: lemon juice, tea, vinegar, chocolate syrup?

Form a Hypothesis

Use pH paper to find the pH values of lemon juice, tea, vinegar, and chocolate syrup. Form a hypothesis to answer the question above. Write your hypothesis in your Science Journal.

Safety

Use care when handling vinegar and lemon juice. Don't get it in your eyes. Do not eat or drink any of the materials. Wash your hands as necessary.

Test Your Hypothesis

1. Think about the materials that have been provided for you. How will you test your hypothesis?
2. Make a list of the steps that you will follow. How will you observe your sample? After you have completed your list, have your teacher approve your plan.
3. Carry out your experiment. Take careful notes about what you observe. You might want to organize your observations in a table like the one on the next page.

Data and Observations

Substance	pH	Observations (when added to milk)
Vinegar		
Lemon juice		
Tea		
Chocolate syrup		

Interpret Your Data

1. Write a description of each of the different solutions that you observed.

_____

_____

_____

_____

Conclude and Apply

1. What was the common factor that caused some solutions to curdle?

_____

_____

_____

_____

2. Was your hypothesis supported? Explain.

_____

_____

_____

_____

Going Further
Do research to find out how allowing milk to curdle is important in the production of both cottage cheese and hard cheese. Write a short research paper about what you learn.

⬤ Inquiry Activity 18 | Cabbage Chemistry

Some materials change color when exposed to an acid or a base. These materials are called indicators. For example, blue litmus paper turns pink in acids. The water in which a red or purple cabbage was cooked also changes color when exposed to an acid or a base. In this activity, you will use cabbage juice as an indicator. The color of cabbage juice will vary from greenish-yellow when mixed with a very strong base to bright red when mixed with a very strong acid.

Possible Materials

- test-tube rack
- test tubes (4)
- labels and pencil
- 25-mL graduated cylinders (4)
- 40 mL red/purple cabbage juice
- stirring rods (3)
- droppers (3)
- vinegar
- dilute ammonia solution
- baking soda solution
- lemon juice

Question

What happens to cabbage juice when each of the following solutions is added to it: vinegar, dilute ammonia solution, baking soda solution?

Form a Hypothesis

Research the properties of vinegar, ammonia, and baking soda. What might cabbage juice do when exposed to them? Make a hypothesis to answer the question. Write your hypothesis in your Science Journal.

Safety 🔪 🥽 👕 🧤 ☣

Some of these solutions are poisonous. Do not taste, eat, or drink any materials used in the lab. Do not inhale vapors from the solutions. These solutions can stain your clothes. Inform your teacher if you come in contact with any of the solutions.

Test Your Hypothesis

1. Think about the materials that have been provided for you. How will you test your hypothesis?
2. Make a list of the steps that you will follow. You'll probably want to put the same amount of cabbage juice in each test tube. What solutions will you add to different tubes? Label each test tube. Remember to keep a control, that is, a sample of cabbage juice to which you do nothing. Once you have completed your list, ask your teacher to approve your plan.
3. Carry out your experiment. Make careful observations and write them in a table like the one on the next page. After you finish, wash your hands with soap and water. Dispose of all solutions as instructed by your teacher.

Data Table

Test Tube	Solution Added to Cabbage Juice	Observations
X	Vinegar	
Y	Ammonia solution	
Z	Baking soda solution	
Control	None	

Interpret Your Data

1. What color did the cabbage juice in each test tube become when the different solutions were added?

   _____

   _____

   _____

2. What was the independent variable in your experiment? What was the dependent variable? What was held constant?

   _____

   _____

   _____

Conclude and Apply

1. Arrange your test tubes according to color (from most red to most green). Include the control as one of the center test tubes. What does this color change represent?

   _____

   _____

   _____

2. Repeat your cabbage juice experiment using lemon juice. Is lemon juice an acid or a base? How do you know?

   _____

   _____

   _____

Going Further

Slowly add some of the ammonia solution to the test tube that you previously used for vinegar and cabbage juice. What happens to the color of the indicator? How can you explain these color changes?

Inquiry Activity 19 | States of Matter

Water exists in three states—solid, liquid, and gas. Solid water is ice. The water molecules in ice vibrate but cannot change position relative to other water molecules. In liquid water, molecules are free to move around each other. However, the molecules remain close together. Gaseous water is called water vapor. Water molecules in vapor have so much energy that they escape the attractions of the other water molecules. Water vapor spreads out into the available space. In this activity, you will investigate the three states of water.

Possible Materials

- 500-mL beaker
- crushed ice
- hot plate
- Celsius thermometer
- graph paper
- ring stand
- thermometer clamp

Question

How does water behave as its temperature is increased?

Form a Hypothesis

Think about the experiences that you've had with the different states of water. Now, make a hypothesis to answer the question above. Write your hypothesis in your Science Journal.

Safety

The hot plate and beaker will be very hot. Do not touch them until after they have cooled.

Test Your Hypothesis

1. Think about the materials that you have been given. How will you test your hypothesis?

2. Make a list of the steps that you will follow. You'll probably want to put crushed ice into the beaker. How will you heat the beaker? How will you measure temperature? How slowly do you need to heat the beaker in order to observe the temperature at which the state changes? Once you have designed your experiment, ask your teacher to approve your plan.

3. Carry out your experiment. Make careful temperature readings at regular time intervals as the water is heated. Note the time when the last piece of ice melts. Also note the time when the water first begins to boil. You might want to record your data in a table like the one on the next page.

Data and Observations

Time (minutes)															
Temperature (°C)															
Observations															

Interpret Your Data

1. Look carefully at your data. At what temperature did the last bit of ice melt? At what temperature did the water first begin to boil?

   _____

   _____

   _____

2. Make a graph showing how the water temperature changed through time. Label the *x*-axis of your graph *Time (min)* and the *y*-axis *Temperature (Celsius)*.

Conclude and Apply

1. Examine the graph that you made. Write a description of how the water temperature changed through the experiment. What was the temperature when the ice was melting? How did the temperature change after the last bit of ice melted? How did the temperature behave when the water began to boil?

   _____

   _____

   _____

2. In this activity, you saw how water changes state. Give some other examples of matter changing state.

   _____

   _____

   _____

   _____

Going Further
Research to find out why water is a good substance to use to cool machinery. What is specific heat? Give a short speech to communicate what you learn.

Inquiry Activity 20 | Isotopes And Atomic Mass

In this activity, you will find out how scientists determine the atomic mass of an element.

Background

Atomic mass is the sum of the number of protons and neutrons in the nucleus of an atom. All of the atoms of an element have the same number of protons in their nuclei, but the number of neutrons can vary. Atoms of the same element with different numbers of neutrons are called isotopes. Most elements have more than one isotope. Isotopes are identified by using the name of the element followed by the mass number of the isotope. Some isotopes also have special names. For example, the three isotopes of hydrogen are hydrogen-1, called protium; hydrogen-2, called deuterium; and hydrogen-3, called tritium. On the periodic table, the atomic mass of an element takes into account all of the isotopes of that element, and how much of each isotope is found in nature.

Possible Materials

- 10 small plastic or paper cups
- black beans
- white beans
- calculator
- periodic table

Question

How can you determine the atomic mass of boron, which is 20% boron-10 and 80% boron-11?

Form a Hypothesis

Think about the number of protons and neutrons in each isotope. How could you use that information to help you make a model of boron? Then, in your Science Journal, write a hypothesis to answer the question above.

Safety 🥽

Do not eat or throw your beans.

Test Your Hypothesis

1. Think about the materials that you have been given. How will you test your hypothesis?
2. Make a list of the steps that you will follow. You'll probably want to use 2 cups to represent boron-10 and eight cups to represent boron-11. How will you use the two different colors of beans? What will each white bean represent? What will each black bean represent? How much mass will one bean represent? Have your teacher approve your plan.
3. Build your model and get your data from it. You might want to use a table like the one on the next page to organize your data.

The Three Isotopes of Hydrogen

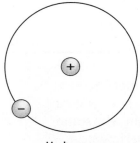

Hydrogen
atomic mass-1

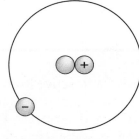

Deuterium
atomic mass-2

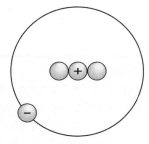

Tritium
atomic mass-3

Data Table

Isotope of boron	Number of atoms represented	Mass number
Boron-10		
Boron-11		

Interpret Your Data

1. With your teacher's help, calculate the atomic mass of boron using a weighted average. Show your work.

2. How does your calculated atomic mass compare to the atomic mass found on the periodic table?

_____

_____

_____

Conclude and Apply

1. If your calculated atomic mass is different from the one in the periodic table, list at least one possible reason for the difference.

_____

_____

_____

2. Write a general procedure for how a scientist would calculate the atomic mass of any element.

_____

_____

_____

_____

Going Further

Some elements have radioactive isotopes. Radioactive isotopes often are used as tracers in scientific experiments. Use research materials to find out what a tracer is and what isotopes are commonly used as tracers. Explain why some isotopes are not suitable for use as tracers in some scientific experiments.

Assessing Activity Work

Activity work can be assessed by observing students as they progress through the different parts of an activity. Both individuals and cooperative groups can be observed and evaluated. In addition to observing, one can ask students questions at different times and evaluate their answers. These strategies will reveal students' levels of understanding of both process and content. With this feedback, it will be possible to detect preconceptions and provide reteaching or plan subsequent goals for a student or an entire group.

Performance Assessment of Science Inquiry Labs

The following elements make these labs suitable for performance assessment tasks. The labs

- allow students to show what they know and what they can do.
- provide opportunities to evaluate the processes involved in completing a task.
- are realistic and thought-provoking.
- stress depth more than breadth and mastery more than speed.

Why Assess Performance?

Assessing performance during science labs is useful for preparing students for a world in which they will have to know fundamental concepts and display basic and higher-level skills. The more they develop critical-thinking and problem-solving skills, the better they will be prepared for the ever-changing future.

Using Performance Task Assessment Lists

Performance Task Assessment Lists can be used for all Science Inquiry Labs and should be used prior to using a Rubric. These lists, used by both students and teachers, provide an objective forum for student assessment. Performance Task Assessment Lists guide students in their work and help them to become independent learners.

Before students begin working, they should read through the appropriate Performance Task Assessment List to become familiar with how the process and/or product will be assessed by both them and their teacher. After their work is completed, students can use the Performance Task Assessment List to judge the quality of their work. Points are assigned to each element on the list based on its importance. Because students know the specific objectives that will be assessed, the teacher receives work that is organized, accurate, and allows for easier assessment. The teacher not only scores the quality of the students' end processes or products, but also scores the quality of students' self-assessments. If a grade is needed, it can be derived form the total points earned on the Performance Task Assessment List.

If students study examples of other students' work that were judged to be excellent by the teacher, students have a much better idea of the level of performance to target. These examples of excellent work together with Performance Task Assessment Lists provide students with direction.

Using Rubrics

Rubrics are used less frequently than Performance Task Assessment Lists to periodically assess the overall quality of student work. After making a series of products, the students are asked how they are doing with reference to the standards of quality, on one type of product.

Specific examples, guidelines, and information about assessment using Performance Task Assessment Lists and Rubrics can be found in Glencoe's *Performance Assessment in the Science Classroom* (PASC) booklet.

Inquiry Activity 1 ....Page 1
It's a Small World

Purpose Students will classify microorganisms according to their physical characteristics.

Inquiry Skills Reinforced asking questions, designing an investigation, conducting an investigation, making observations, analyzing data, classifying, communicating

Time required one class period

Background Microorganisms are classified into different subgroups. During this lab, students will observe many types of protists, which include the protozoa (mostly animal-like protists) and the algae (photosynthesizing protists). Students also might observe organisms (or portions of organisms) representing the animal or plant kingdoms.

Protozoa are classified mainly by general appearance, and further by means of locomotion.

The 60,000 species of protozoa are divided as follows:
1. *Flagellates* – locomote by means of flagella; some can photosynthesize and some feed in an animal-like fashion
2. *Sarcodina*– includes the amoebae; locomote by means of flowing cytoplasm; envelope and ingest prey
3. *Sporozoans* – move by bending and gliding; most are intracellular parasites
4. *Ciliates* – locomote by beating the water with their legions of cilia; includes *Paramecium*

Diatoms are unicellular algae containing green chlorophyll pigment for photosynthesis. They are a major component of plankton, live in freshwater and salt water, and are usually encased in silica shells. They are among the most abundant life-forms on Earth.

Students also may see nematodes (microscopic worms) and microscopic crustaceans such as *Daphnia* or *Macrothrix*. You might want to have a biology text with photographs available for students' reference.

While considering how these organisms fit into the food chain, students might correctly conclude that they are food for very small fish. However, you might mention that even the blue whale, the largest known living animal, strains plankton out of the sea for food.

Possible Procedure Divide students into groups of about three, depending on availability of microscopes. Supply them with some prepared slides, but also allow them to make at least a few of their own slides from pond water or from prepared solutions containing known microorganisms.

Preparation Tips
- Students may be asked to bring in jars of pond water; or, a culture of dried leaves with water should yield some microorganisms.
- Live specimens and prepared slides can be ordered through a biological science supplier.
- Students should be cautioned about the dangers of glass slides, and should be told to wash their hands thoroughly throughout the experiment.

Interpret Your Data
1. Students might notice that some microorganisms are plant-like and others animal-like.
2. See *Background*.

Conclude and Apply
1. Students might classify things into "worm-like creatures," "crab-like creatures," "blob-like creatures," etc. This is actually very close to how scientists classify them.
2. All microorganisms are an important link in the food chain, and diatoms and other photosynthesizing microorganisms are major producers of oxygen.

Going Further Students might find interesting facts about the various groups of microorganisms. For example, some flagellates live symbiotically in the guts of termites and wood roaches.

Inquiry Activity 2 ....Page 3
Designing a Classification System

Purpose Students will learn about taxonomy by classifying 15 common animals.

Inquiry Skills Reinforced making observations, analyzing data, classifying, forming conclusions, communicating

Time Required one class period for performing the activity and a portion of a second period for sharing results

Possible Procedure Student groups examine the animal pictures and record their knowledge and observations. Students should pay close attention to physical characteristics including skeletal structure, skin and hair, and appendages. Students should group similar animals and separate dissimilar animals.

Preparation Tips
- Students will benefit from a brief discussion about why and how things are classified before they conduct the activity.
- You might want to provide each group with a photocopy of the pictures.

Interpret Your Data
1. Answers will vary. Some possible answers include the following: animals with gills are fish; animals with beaks have wings; animals with exoskeletons are insects and spiders.
2. Student classifications will vary depending on category criteria. Accept all logical classifications.

Conclude and Apply
1. Students choose an additional animal to add to their classification system. Answers will vary, but students should demonstrate how the new animal is similar to and different from existing animal categories.

Going Further Students should choose a group of similar animals and research the scientific names of each (example: wolf, dog, coyote, fox). In most cases, the genus name will be the same for some of the animals. For example: *Canis* lupis (gray wolf), *Canis* familiaris (domestic dog), and *Canis* latrans (North American coyote). For some animals, the genus name might be different. For example: *Vulpes* vulpes (red fox). Students might conclude that the gray wolf, North American coyote, and domestic dog are more closely related to each other than to the red fox. Students also might want to examine higher levels of taxonomy such as family, order, and class.

Inquiry Activity 3 ....Page 5
Effects of Acid Rain

Purpose Students will acquire a fundamental understanding of the nature of acid rain, why it occurs, and some possible consequences of acid rain.

Inquiry Skills Reinforced forming hypotheses, testing hypotheses, graphing, measuring, describing, comparing and contrasting, collecting data, communicating

Time Required one-half period to set up the activity; five to ten minutes per day for care of plants and observations; one period for final measurements and analyzing data

Background The pH of a solution is defined as the negative, base-ten logarithm of the hydrogen ion concentration. Because of the logarithmic function, each number change in pH represents a tenfold change in the concentration of hydrogen ions. For example, a solution with a pH of three contains ten times more hydrogen ions per unit volume than a solution with a pH of four.

Acid rain forms because of emissions of sulfur oxides and nitrogen oxides from automobiles and power plants. These compounds react with water in Earth's atmosphere to form sulfuric acid and nitric acid, respectively. These acids lower the pH of rainwater below its normal pH (about 5.6) to produce acid rain.

Possible Procedure Students nearly fill two large pots with potting soil. Two or three corn seeds are planted in each pot and watered with normal rainwater until the seedlings emerge from the soil. A solution that will represent acid rain is prepared by mixing vinegar into water until a pH of about four is obtained. This pH is commonly observed in natural acid rain events. One pot is watered with normal rainwater. The other is watered with "acid rain." Students record the height and condition of plants at regular intervals.

Preparation Tips
- Corn can be purchased locally or through supply catalogs. Because of the fungicide that is applied to seeds, students should wash their hands after handling them.
- If you want to use a different type of plant, make certain that the plant grows best in basic soil. For example, corn prefers soil with a pH of about 7.0–7.5.
- Most brands of potting soil should work well for this activity.
- Some soils contain abundant calcite. These soils will neutralize any acid applied to them for some period of time. You can test soil for calcite by applying a drop of 10% HCl to the soil. If the soil fizzes, it contains calcite.
- Students might ask how corn manages to grow in natural rainwater (pH=5.6). Tell them that corn plants are not damaged by natural rainwater and that many soils easily buffer its effects. However, very acidic rain will damage the plants and might overwhelm the soil's ability to buffer the pH.

Interpret Your Data
1. Check to make certain that students correctly graph the data in their tables.
2. Students probably will find that the line representing the plants watered with rainwater rises more steeply than the line representing the plants watered with "acid rain."

Conclude and Apply
1. Acid rain could damage corn crops unless the soil is able to neutralize the acid. Damaged plants yield less corn.
2. The lime neutralizes the acids that fall onto the field in rain.

Going Further Help students understand the importance of peer review to science.

Inquiry Activity 4 ....Page 7
Growth Rings as Indicators of Climate

Purpose Students will learn that growth rings in tree trunks can be used to reconstruct past climate.

Inquiry Skills Reinforced asking questions, designing an experiment, conducting an experiment, analyzing data, communicating

Time Required one class period

Background The science of using tree rings to learn about past climatic conditions is called dendroclimatology. Scientists in this field analyze tree-ring width and cell characteristics. Because many factors can affect the thickness of tree rings, stands of trees must be selected carefully. For example, researchers are more likely to learn about past precipitation patterns from trees that are growing in relatively dry climates. In dry climates, the amount of rainfall limits tree growth. In high latitude regions, temperature is likely to be the factor that limits tree growth.

Possible Procedure Students count the number of rings in Figures 2, 3, and 4, and record these data in a table. Students also use a metric ruler to measure the widths of the various rings in each figure. They record the years that are represented by the widest and narrowest rings in the table. These data then can be used to discern which years received the most and least rainfall.

Preparation Tips
- Review with students the proper way to use a metric ruler.
- If your students have difficulty working with low differences in ring width, you can enlarge the drawings with a copying machine.
- Remind your students that ring width is measured perpendicular to the ring boundaries.

Interpret Your Data
1. The age of the trees represented by Figure 2 and Figure 3 is eight years. The age for Figure 4 is six years.

Conclude and Apply
1. The tree in Figure 2 received the most rain during 2002. It received the least rain during 2000. The tree in Figure 3 received the most rain during 1999 and 2002. It received the least rain during 2000. The tree in Figure 4 received the most rain during 2000. It received the least rain during 1999. The widest ring represents the year with the highest precipitation, and the narrowest ring represents the year with the least precipitation.
2. The location represented by the tree in Figure 4 had conditions that were best suited for growth. The tree trunk in Figure 4 is the same width as the tree trunks in the other figures, but it has fewer growth rings. Therefore, it had a higher average growth rate.

Going Further Crossdating is the technique by which similar patterns of tree rings are matched from one tree or wood sample to another. Crossdating allows the tree-ring chronology to be extended back in time. For example, a modern tree can be compared to an older fallen log. If the lifetimes of the two trees overlapped, similar ring patterns can be correlated, providing a known age in the fallen log. The ages of older rings then can be determined in the log.

Inquiry Activity 5 ....Page 9
Radiation and Its Effects on Seeds

Purpose Students will observe and record the effects of radiation on the growth patterns of seedlings.

Inquiry Skills Reinforced designing an experiment, conducting an experiment, graphing, analyzing data, predicting, communicating

Time Required 30–40 minutes for initial set up; after sprouting, 5–10 minutes of class time at regular intervals to observe and record data; 30 minutes for concluding activity and cleaning up

Background Irradiated seeds that are purchased from supply houses have been exposed to varying amounts of gamma radiation, which causes random mutations to occur in the genetic material stored in the seeds. Some of these mutations will produce a visible effect in the seedlings. Most mutations will be detrimental to the plants.

Preparation Tips
- Ask students to work in groups of 3 or 4 to perform this investigation.
- Irradiated seeds pose no risk to students because the seeds themselves are not radioactive. However, if you have any reservations about the reaction of some parents, send home information letters and permission slips.
- Seeds that have been exposed to different amounts of radiation are available from science suppliers. If you cannot obtain seeds from a supply house, you might want to request that your dentist or doctor expose seeds using an X-ray machine. Place seeds in carefully labeled plastic bags, and have them irradiated for different periods of time ranging from 0–30 seconds.
- Students should be made aware that uniformity of time intervals between collection of data is important for getting valid results.

Possible Procedure Students fill three or four small containers with potting soil. The containers are labeled according to the amount of radiation that the seeds to be planted in them have received. Plant three to five seeds of the appropriate type in each container. Each container should receive the same amount of water, and the soil should be kept moist. Students record the height and condition of seedlings at regular intervals in a data table.

Interpret Your Data
1. Check to make certain that students correctly graph the data in their tables. A graph title, legend, and appropriate axis labels should be present on students' graphs.
2. Students probably will find that the line representing the plants that received no radiation rises more steeply than the lines representing plants that received varying amounts of radiation. Other comparisons include number of leaves, leaf shape, and color.

Conclude and Apply
1. Answers will vary.
2. Students should conclude that similar malformations might occur in the root system. They could test their conclusions by carefully extracting some of the seedlings and comparing their root systems.

Going Further Students design a similar experiment using microwaves. High-energy radiation, such as gamma radiation, tends to cause genetic mutations, whereas microwaves cause molecules to vibrate and produce heat. Seeds exposed to microwaves should not exhibit the same types of effects seen in the plants grown from gamma-irradiated seeds. However, sufficient exposure to microwaves will render the seeds nonviable.

Inquiry Activity 6 ....Page 11
Survival in Extreme Climates

Purpose Students will learn how cactus plants are adapted to survive in a harsh desert climate.

Inquiry Skills Reinforced asking questions, designing an experiment, conducting an experiment, making observations, measuring, analyzing data, forming conclusions, communicating

Time required one class period

Background Animal environmental adaptations are both behavioral and structural, whereas plant adaptations are only structural. Structures that help the cactus survive in the desert include the following:

- Spines, instead of leaves, that deter desert predators from eating the plant;
- A thick stem, often with ribs that direct rainfall directly down to the base of the plant;
- Extremely large root systems that grow close to the surface of the soil and provide maximum access to water from dew, mists, or light rainfall;
- A waxy, thick covering that holds water within the plant;
- A tough exterior (generally) that is able to withstand extended periods of direct sunlight without damage; and
- A round or otherwise compact shape that provides a relatively small surface area from which water can transpire into the atmosphere.

A large saguaro cactus (one of the typical southwestern United States varieties) can have a root system up to 50 feet long. Almost 90 percent of a cactus is water, and the plant can sustain a 60 percent loss of water and still survive.

Possible Procedure Students may be divided into groups of 2 or 3 to facilitate discussion. They should examine the characteristics of each plant and record their observations. Some enterprising students may decide to simulate rainfall to see how their plants channel the water. This could lead them to some of the characteristics listed in *Background* above.

Preparation Tips
- Students may be asked to bring potted plants from home.
- Inexpensive house plants, including cacti, may be purchased at a local gardening store.
- Be sure to warn students about the dangers of cactus needles; you may wish to require the use of safety goggles and gloves.

Interpret Your Data
1. Responses should reflect some of the unique characteristics listed in *Background* above.

Conclude and Apply
1. Conclusions should follow logically from differences listed in *Interpret Your Data*. One insightful response could be that, because cacti have needles instead of leaves, no rainfall is wasted; after a light rain, some water may be left on the broad leaves of a plant, while in the case of a cactus, all of the water is directed down to the root system.

Going Further Answers will vary depending on what environment is researched. Answers could include, for example, grasses in heavily forested areas that are adapted to require low levels of sunlight to flourish, or vines in a rain forest that wind around trees to enormous heights so that their leaves can reach the sunlight that the tall trees would otherwise block.

Purpose Students will learn to distinguish anticlines and synclines.

Inquiry Skills Reinforced asking questions, designing an experiment, conducting an experiment, making models, analyzing data, communicating

Time Required one class period for activity; additional time for *Going Further*

Background Anticlines are folds in which the rock layers have been folded up in the middle. When looking at the front edge of an anticline, one sees the upward-arching rock layers. However, it often is not possible to see a slice through an anticline on Earth's surface. Therefore, it is necessary to recognize anticlines from the arrangement of the rock layers that make up Earth's surface. The rock layers of an eroded anticline will form parallel stripes on Earth's surface. The oldest rock will be at the center of the anticline. Rock layers get younger away from the center.

Synclines are folds in which the rock layers have been folded down in the middle. When looking at the front of a syncline, one sees downward arching rocks. On Earth's eroded surface, the rock layers in a syncline will form parallel stripes similar to an anticline. However, the youngest rock layer will be in the center. Rock layers get progressively older away from the center. Students may find these concepts perplexing until they finish making the models described in this activity. Upon completing the models, they should understand these relationships completely.

Possible Procedures Students make two different flat stacks of clay. Each stack should include four different-colored layers of clay and should be about 10 cm long and 7 cm wide. They should make each clay layer about 1–2 cm thick. Using the principle of superposition, they record the color of the clay layers from oldest to youngest in the table provided. Students fold the first stack into an anticline by bending each end down. They fold the second stack into a syncline by bending each end up. Students use the plastic knife to cut through the anticline near its base. This models erosion of the anticline. Students look down from the top onto "Earth's surface" to see that the oldest clay layer is in the center of the anticline, and the other layers get younger away from the center. Students use the plastic knife to cut through the syncline model. Students look down on the model to see that the youngest layer is in the center and that the other layers get older away from the center.

Preparation Tips
- Students might need help getting started.
- You might want to spread paper over tables or desks to make cleanup easier.

Interpret Your Data
1. See *Background*.

Conclude and Apply
1. Students should indicate that an anticline is an upfold and a syncline is a downfold. The oldest rock layer is in the center of an anticline. The youngest rock layer appears on each side farthest from the center. The youngest rock layer is at the center of a syncline. The oldest rock layer appears on each side farthest from the center.
2. An anticline would have the oldest rock layer in the center. A syncline would have the youngest rock layer in the center.

Going Further Oil often is trapped in anticlines. During exploration, a variety of techniques is used to identify these rock structures at the surface and in the subsurface.

Inquiry Activity 8
Making Waves

Purpose Students will derive the relationship between grain size and beach slope.

Inquiry Skills Reinforced asking questions, designing an investigation, conducting an investigation, analyzing data, making calculations, graphing, predicting

Time Required one period to conduct the activity; one period to analyze data and make graphs

Background Beach slope varies with the mean grain size of the sand and with wave energy. Mean grain size has a much larger effect than wave energy. Beaches with larger grain sizes will have steeper slopes. For example, a beach with a grain size of about 2 mm should have a slope of about 40°. Beaches with a grain size of 0.25 mm should have a slope of about 1° to 4°. If grain size is held constant, beach slope will increase as wave energy decreases.

Possible Procedure Students form a coarse-sand "beach" in one tub and a fine-sand "beach" in a second tub. Students slowly pour an appropriate amount of water into each tub. After a few minutes, students use a short section of board to make waves in one tub for about 10 minutes. This should be done by moving the board slowly between two marked points on each tub. These points should be about 10 cm apart and should be as far from the beach as equipment allows. Students repeat the procedure in the second tub, taking care to use about the same amount of wave energy. Students then trace the profile of each beach on the side of the tubs. The tubs are emptied, and the slope is measured using a protractor.

Preparation Tips
- Sand of various grain sizes can be obtained at many hardware suppliers, concrete plants, and aggregate plants. Natural sand also can be used. Use clean sand that does not contain silt and clay. Coarse sand should be about 2 mm. Fine sand should be less than 0.5 mm.
- To reduce the amount of materials needed, you might want to conduct this investigation as a class project.
- Line a cardboard box with plastic. Use this box for discarded sand. Don't overfill.

Interpret Your Data
1. The coarse beach should have the higher slope angle. The difference will vary with experimental design.
2. Help students start measuring grains. Students will need to estimate sizes smaller than 1 mm.
3. Students' graphs should show that beach slope increases linearly with grain size.

Conclude and Apply
1. Students should realize that the slope of a beach increases as grain size increases.
2. Students could determine the grain size of the unknown sample and then use their graphs to estimate the beach slope.

Going Further Beaches are important ecologically and also are important for recreation. One of the biggest problems occurring on beach-front property is beach erosion. The United States has funded many studies about beach erosion and other concerns.

Purpose Students will learn how linear speed varies with latitude on Earth. This is an important concept because it provides a foundation for understanding the Coriolis effect.

Inquiry Skills Reinforced designing an experiment, conducting an experiment, collecting data, making calculations, analyzing data, communicating

Time Required one period to conduct investigation; Additional time might be needed for the *Going Further* exercise.

Background Linear speed is a measure of how fast a point on Earth's surface is moving through space because of Earth's rotation. Linear speed is greatest at Earth's equator and decreases toward Earth's poles. It is exactly zero at the poles. The change in linear speed with latitude can be used to explain the Coriolis effect to students. Imagine a parcel of air traveling north from the equator. The air is moving to the east at the same linear speed as a point on Earth's equator. As the air moves north over land that is moving east at a lower linear speed, it appears to curve to the right. Similar reasoning can be used to explain why an air mass moving south in the northern hemisphere would curve to the right. Because Earth also possesses angular velocity, an air mass moving east to west or west to east in the northern hemisphere also will turn to the right. However, this latter concept will be too advanced for most middle-school students to understand completely. Students will have to accept on faith that all moving air and ocean currents turn to the right north of the equator and to the left south of the equator.

Possible Procedure Students put small pieces of tape, as markers, on the Prime Meridian at the equator, 30°N latitude, 60°N latitude, and the north pole. They align the markers with the support frame of the globe, as shown in the illustration on the student page. Using their fingers, they slowly rotate the globe west to east for 1 s. For each latitude, using string and a meterstick, they measure the distance from the prime meridian to the support frame and record their data. The procedure is repeated, rotating for 2 s and for 3 s. Students then calculate the speed of each latitude for each trial. These values will not all be the same and are not equal to Earth's true linear speeds. The exercise simply illustrates that linear speed decreases toward the poles. Students will calculate the true values for Earth in *Conclude and Apply*.

Preparation Tip The globe should be mounted on a frame that can be used as a reference.

Interpret Your Data
1. Linear speed decreases with increasing latitude. It is zero at the poles.

Conclude and Apply
1. Distances should be about 40,075 km at the equator, 34,647 km at 30°N, 19,983 km at 60°N, and 0 km at the north pole.
2. 24 hours = 86,400 s; divide each value above by 86,400 s to get the following speeds: equator: 0.46 km/s; 30°N: 0.40 km/s; 60°N: 0.23 km/s; and at the north pole: 0 km/s.

Going Further Students should realize that a basic scientific understanding often can be used to explain many phenomena.

Purpose Students will observe and describe diatom microfossils.

Inquiry Skills Reinforced asking questions, designing an experiment, conducting an experiment, making observations, describing, analyzing data, communicating

Time Required one class period for activity; one or two class periods for *Going Further*

Background Diatoms are a unicellular, photosynthetic algae that produce silicified cell walls. The cells commonly range from 50 microns to 200 microns, although they can be smaller or larger. Each cell produces a silicified cell wall, or shell, called a frustule that is made of opaline silica. The shell has two valves that overlap similar to the way that the lid to a petri dish overlaps the bottom. Under favorable conditions, diatom shells can "rain down" on the floor of the ocean or a lake to form diatomite.

Possible Procedures Students use a small spatula to put a small amount (it only takes a light sprinkle; using too much will make viewing difficult) of diatomite on a small piece of black construction paper. Students might want to make trays from black construction paper in advance. Black is an ideal color because the diatoms will stand out. Students examine the diatoms under a stereomicroscope. The microfossils can be manipulated using an ultra-fine artist's paintbrush. Students describe and draw what they observe.

Preparation Tips
- If inhaled in large amounts, diatomite can irritate the respiratory tract. To ensure safety, do not pour from the bag in the classroom. A small amount of diatomite can be transferred into the bottom of a watch glass in a well-ventilated area. The watch glass can be brought into the classroom. This will be more than enough material for even the largest group of students.
- Diatomite can be obtained from most aquarium or pet shops. It is used for aquarium filters.
- Ultra-fine brushes can be obtained at most art supply stores. If ultra-fine brushes cannot be obtained, cut the majority of hairs from normal artist's paint brushes.

Interpret Your Data
1. Student descriptions should include size, shape, color, and any surface ornamentation on the microfossils.

Conclude and Apply
1. Diatomite forms in the ocean and in some freshwater lakes. Diatom organisms in surface waters produce shells. When the diatoms die, the shells fall to the floor of the ocean or lake. These fossils can accumulate to great thickness to form sediment. Ocean sediment can be uplifted above sea level along coastal areas. Ancient lake beds can be exposed by erosion.
2. Scientists learn about the types of organisms that lived in the ocean or a lake long ago. Some microfossils are the only evidence of extinct species or groups. Because many types of organisms only live in waters with a certain temperature range, microfossils provide information about past ocean temperatures. Other answers also could be acceptable.

Going Further A wide variety of microfossils exist. These include fossils produced by algae, bacteria, and protists, as well as small fossils from plants and animals. The most common ocean sediments produced by microfossils are oozes made from siliceous shells or calcium-carbonate shells. Chalk is a common rock that consists largely of calcium-carbonate microfossils.

Inquiry Activity 11..................Page 21
Coal: What's My Rank?

Purpose Students will learn about the properties, formation, and importance of coal.

Inquiry Skills Reinforced Forming hypotheses, making observations, using tables, analyzing data, making models, predicting, communicating

Time Required one class period for performing the activity; Additional time might be needed for research and to complete the *Going Further* exercise.

Background Coal is commonly classified according to its rank. Lignite is the lowest-rank coal. Lignite is a soft, brown coal that might contain some recognizable plant material. The next higher rank is subbituminous coal. This type of coal contains more highly altered plant material and is transitional to bituminous coal. Bituminous coal is a moderately hard, black, brittle coal. Anthracite is the highest-rank coal. It is a hard, black, shiny coal that often breaks with conchoidal fracture (smooth, curving fracture).

Possible Procedure Student groups examine samples of lignite, subbituminous, bituminous, and anthracite coal and record their observations in a table. Students should pay close attention to hardness, fracture, color, and other properties. A penny can be used to assess the hardness of the different coal samples. Hardness can be recorded in relative terms, such as soft, hard, hardest, etc. Fracture can be determined by examining surfaces on the coal samples.

Preparation Tips
- Samples of the different types of coal can be purchased from supply houses.
- You might want to have soap and towels available so that students can wash after the activity.

Interpret Your Data
1. Hardness should increase with the rank of the coal samples (lignite < subbituminous < bituminous < anthracite). Lignite coal breaks randomly. Subbituminous and bituminous coal break with brittle fracture or along bedding planes. Anthracite coal breaks with conchoidal fracture.
2. Students should be able to correctly classify each sample according to rank.

Conclude and Apply
1. The coal becomes harder and more dense. The color changes from a brown or brownish-black to black. The coal changes from friable to having brittle fracture to having conchoidal fracture.
2. The lignite coal will become subbituminous coal, then bituminous coal, then anthracite coal.

Going Further Student posters should show peat forming in a swamp, burial by sediment, conversion to coal, and metamorphism to form anthracite coal.

Inquiry Activity 12.....................Page 23
Tornado in a Jar

Purpose Students will model a tornado.

Inquiry Skills Reinforced asking questions, designing an experiment, making models, conducting an experiment, analyzing data, communicating

Time Required one class period to perform activity; additional time for *Going Further*

Background The strongest tornadoes form from supercells, which are large convective storms containing a mesocyclone. A mesocyclone is a rotating column of air inside of the storm cloud. Mesocyclones often have diameters greater than ten kilometers. These rotating columns of air form because of wind shear in the storm cloud. Under some circumstances, the rotating air can be tilted into a nearly vertical position. It then can narrow and extend toward the ground. As the column narrows, its speed of rotation increases. A wall cloud, which is a dark cloud beneath the main thunderstorm, forms and a funnel cloud can emerge from it. A tornado occurs if the funnel reaches the ground.

Possible Procedures Students fill the jar three-fourths of the way full with water. They then add the soap, vinegar, and food coloring. Students screw on the lid and swirl the jar in a counter-clockwise motion. Students should observe a vortex inside the jar.

Preparation Tips
- Large peanut butter jars work well for this activity.
- Tell your students not to use too much food coloring. Too much color can make it difficult to see the vortex.
- Remind your students that lids need to be screwed on tightly.

Interpret Your Data
1. Students should observe a vortex of spinning water inside of the jar. If the jar was rotated with a counter-clockwise motion, the sense of rotation of the water vortex will be the same as in most tornadoes.

Conclude and Apply
1. Answers will vary. Possible answers include the following. A spinning vortex that is similar to the spinning vortex of air that comprises a tornado was produced inside the jar. The water vortex spins much more slowly than a tornado does.
2. The column of air rotates faster as it narrows. This occurs because angular momentum is conserved. When the radius of the column of air decreases, it must spin faster to keep angular momentum constant.

Going Further Much research is being conducted to learn more about how tornadoes develop. This research includes field studies, computer modeling, and studies using Doppler radar. The research is important because it might enable forecasters to better predict when and where a tornado will occur. Most of this research is being funded by the United States government. Agencies such as the National Severe Storms Laboratory and the National Weather Service are involved in tornado research. Many university faculty and students also are working to better understand how tornadoes develop.

Inquiry Activity 13......................Page 25
Identifying Metals and Nonmetals

Purpose Students will identify metals and nonmetals using a conductivity tester.

Inquiry Skills Reinforced asking questions, designing an experiment, conducting an experiment, making observations, collecting data, analyzing data, communicating

Time Required one class period

Background The electrical conductivity of a substance is determined by how tightly the valence electrons are bound. For example, elements in the leftmost column of the periodic table are among the metals. On the other hand, some of the newest superconductors (superconductors have zero resistance) are made of ceramic material. Thus, the use of electrical conductivity as the sole criterion for classifying a substance as a metal is somewhat simplified. Metals are elements that usually are shiny-surfaced, conduct heat and electricity well, can be hammered into thin sheets, and can be drawn into wires. In addition, electrical conductivity depends on the voltage: at 1.5 volts, air is not a conductor of electricity, but under lightning conditions (millions of volts), it is.

Preparation Tips
- The unknown sample must be composed of only one substance. Charcoal is a good sample for a nonmetal. Aluminum foil is a good sample for a metal.
- You may wish to provide small boards for mounting the conductivity-tester apparatus.
- If your wires don't have exposed ends, strip about 2 cm of the insulation from the ends before giving them to the students.
- Emphasize that physical properties of substances can be used for identification and classification.
- Be sure that students know that electrical conductivity indicates that an electric current will pass through an object.

Interpret Your Data
1. Zinc, copper, and iron are metals. The bulb lights.
2. Glass, rubber, and wood are nonmetals. The bulb does not light.
3. Students should observe that metals are shiny and are not brittle.

Conclude and Apply
1. Answers will vary with sample. Conductivity should be the principal identifying characteristic of the unknown sample.

Going Further Electrical conductivity makes metals useful for wiring and electrical contacts. Metals are used in lightning arrestors. Uninsulated metals should not be used around an area where electrical shock could result, such as an aluminum ladder where it might come in contact with electrical lines. Student posters could illustrate the above information with images and captions.

The Inside Story of Packaging

Purpose Students will learn that different types of products require different types of packaging materials and strategies. They also will gain some appreciation for the importance of recycling.

Inquiry Skills Reinforced designing an experiment, conducting an experiment, analyzing data, forming conclusions, communicating

Time Required one class period

Background The six numerical categories for recyclable plastics correspond to the six main resins used in container manufacture. Each resin has its own particular cost and performance advantages, and each can be recycled into various plastic products.

1. Polyethylene terephthalate: strong, stiff and clear; used in plastic soft drink bottles; recycled into carpet fiber and lumber
2. High-density polyethylene: milky-white plastic, strong and chemical resistant; used in detergent bottles; recycled into floor tile
3. Polyvinyl chloride: versatile and chemical resistant; used in clear food packaging and shampoo bottles; recycled into air bubble cushioning
4. Low-density polyethylene: low cost; used in plastic bags of all kinds; recycled into mud flaps, garbage can liners
5. Polypropylene: tough, resistant to oil; used in ketchup and margarine containers; recycled into battery cables and oil funnels
6. Polystyrene: low cost, clear, has insulation properties; used in CD cases, plastic utensils; recycled into light-switch plates and insulation

Possible Procedure Before the day of this activity, students may be instructed to bring various food packages from home. Ask them to have their parents thoroughly wash out the packages. For safety reasons, packages for detergents or other household chemicals should be brought by the teacher, and these should be thoroughly washed and rinsed.

Students can be divided into groups of 3 or 4. Appropriate responses for "Physical Properties" (see data table) of the packages involve things such as shape, color and hardness. Data from each group could be used in a teacher-facilitated brainstorming exercise. The class could then work toward the answers to *Interpret Your Data* and *Conclude and Apply*.

Preparation Ask students and colleagues in advance to save containers from home to be used during this activity.

Interpret Your Data
1. See *Background* for information. There will be some crossover in utility for the various codes of plastics.
2. Examples of appropriate answers: (a) containers coded "1" are generally stiffer than those coded "2," and (b) some containers within a numerical code category are colored, while others are clear or slightly milky in appearance.

Conclude and Apply
1. While there may be some crossover in the uses of these resins, potentially dangerous chemicals will normally be found in packages coded "2." A question that may be asked to guide students to a conclusion is, "Which container would have a better chance to survive being dropped from a great height, a '1' classification or a '2'?"
2. Light-sensitive materials such as hydrogen peroxide would be stored in a pigmented package. Drinking water appears pure and clean in a clear container.

Going Further See the *Background* section. Also, a truck can carry over 2 million plastic bags, but only 500,000 paper grocery bags. Recycled plastic is also burned for fuel in "Waste-To-Energy" plants across the United States. You might want to emphasize to students that recycling technology developed in response to societal needs: reducing waste and conserving material.

Inquiry Activity 15.....................Page 29
Lenses that Magnify

Purpose Students will discover that the focal length of a lens decreases with increasing lens curvature and that the magnifying power of a lens increases as its curvature increases.

Inquiry Skills Reinforced Forming hypotheses, testing hypotheses, interpreting scientific illustrations, comparing and contrasting, communicating

Time Required one class period

Background When an object is placed between the focal point and the lens, its image is magnified. The image is virtual (no light passes through it; it cannot be seen on a screen) and right-side-up. To see the relationship between curvature and magnification, it is sufficient to estimate the image size. Students may place a ruler against the lens or they may try to see the real page and the magnified image at the same time and estimate how many times larger the image appears.

Possible Procedure Students assemble the materials as shown in the figure on the student page. A flashlight is held several meters away from the lens, and its beam is directed at the lens. Students move the lens until a sharp, focused beam of light appears on the index card. Students then measure the focal length. For question 2 in *Interpret Your Data,* students should view type on a page with two lenses of vastly different curvature. Students should estimate which lens has the higher magnification.

Preparation Tips
- High-quality lenses with various focal lengths can be purchased from supply catalogs. Obtain lenses with significantly different focal lengths.
- Students might have a difficult time determining the amount of curvature of their lenses. For lenses with the same diameter, a thicker lens will have greater curvature. Students should be able to determine relative thickness without difficulty.

Interpret Your Data
1. The greater the curvature, the lower the focal length.
2. The greater the curvature, the higher the magnification.

Conclude and Apply
1. The lens with a focal length of 5 cm will have greater curvature.
2. Yes; the semi-round shape of the water drop acts as a convex lens.

Going Further Fresnel (pronounced FRA nel) lenses are flat magnifiers. They consist of a flat side and a ridged side. The ridged side consists of concentric rings that reflect and refract light to produce an image. These magnifiers are very thin and require less material to produce.

Inquiry Activity 16.....................Page 31
Electrolytes and Conductivity

Purpose Students will construct a simple conductivity tester to determine how surface area of electrodes affects the current flow through an electrolytic solution.

Inquiry Skills Reinforced asking questions, forming hypotheses, testing hypotheses, analyzing data, predicting, communicating

Time Required one class period

Background Electrical current is the flow of ions or electrons. An electrode (in this case, the folded aluminum strip) is a conductor inserted into an electrolyte. Conductivity, the opposite of electrical resistance, is the ability of the electrolyte to conduct electricity. The electrical current in the salt water is caused by the dissociation of the sodium chloride into ions. The chloride ions are negatively charged and move from the negative electrode toward the positive electrode. The sodium ions are positively charged and move in the opposite direction.

Bubbles appear at the electrodes as some of the water molecules are split into hydrogen and oxygen molecules. The hydrogen is at the negative electrode and is more noticeable than the oxygen, which is at the positive electrode.

$P = IE,$ where P = electrical power, brightness of the bulb
I = electrical current
E = voltage

The voltage is 3 V throughout the experiment. The current increases as the electrode area increases or the water path length decreases.

Possible Procedure Students construct a conductivity tester as shown in the diagram. The order of the batteries and the lightbulb doesn't matter, but the batteries must be connected in series (positive to negative). Students record the submerged length of the marked electrode and the corresponding brightness of the flashlight bulb.

Preparation Tips
- Battery holders may be purchased or made from pasteboard and brass paper fasteners. Alternatively (but less satisfactorily), students may make the electrode-to-battery, battery-to-battery, and battery-to-lightbulb connections with wires and electrician's tape.
- To make a battery holder for a D cell, cut an "H" shape from a piece of pasteboard such as a cereal box. Each leg of the "H" shape should be 125 mm high and 33 mm wide. The crossbar of the "H" should be 33 mm wide and 60 mm high. Poke holes in the centers of the four tabs of the "H"-shaped piece of pasteboard. Put brass paper fasteners through the two holes on each end of the box. The heads of the paper fasteners should be inside the box, and the legs on the outside. Label one end "+" and the other "−".
- A purchased bulb socket may be used.
- When only 2 cm of the marked electrode is submerged, the bulb may not be lit at all.

Interpret Your Data
1. The longest submerged electrode length should produce the brightest light (provided the electrodes don't touch each other).

Conclude and Apply
1. The bright glow of the flashlight bulb indicated a closed circuit.
2. The increasing brightness of the bulb indicated that more current was flowing as more of the electrode was submerged.
3. The light gets brighter.

Going Further A decrease in the distance between the electrodes increases the conductivity, which increases the electrical current, which increases the brightness of the bulb.

Inquiry Activity 17......................Page 33
Curds and Whey

Purpose Students will observe and describe an effect that is dependent upon pH—the curdling of milk.

Skills Reinforced asking questions, designing an experiment, conducting an experiment, making observations, describing, analyzing data, communicating

Time Required one class period for the activity and one period for answering questions; Additional time might be needed for the *Going Further*.

Background Milk is a colloid. A colloid consists of microscopic particles evenly dispersed in a fluid. The particles in milk consist of aggregated molecules of casein, which is the principle protein in milk. At high pH, the protein aggregates have negative surface charge and repel each other. As the pH is lowered, the amount of negative charge decreases. When a pH value called the isoelectric point is reached, the protein has no net charge and coagulation to form curds occurs. For milk, the isoelectric point is about pH = 4.6. However, some coagulation might occur as the pH approaches this value. Milk can curdle naturally when certain types of bacteria convert lactose to lactic acid, which lowers the pH of the milk.

Possible Procedures Students will pour 50 mL of milk into four plastic cups. They will slowly add vinegar, tea, lemon juice, and diluted chocolate syrup to separate cups. Students should add the substances to the milk slowly and note how much liquid, by volume, has been added. Students should know the pH of each substance. Students stir occasionally and watch for the formation of curds. They also might want to record the pH of the final solution.

Preparation Tips
- All acids can be irritating to the eyes, so students should wear goggles and use care when handling them.
- Keep milk refrigerated to prevent premature curdling.

- pH paper can be purchased through supply catalogs. It is relatively inexpensive.

Interpret Your Data
1. Students' descriptions should indicate whether the milk curdled. Students also might list other observations that they made, such as a change in color or consistency. The milk in the cups that had vinegar or lemon juice added to them should curdle. It is possible that some slight curdling might occur in the cup that had tea added to it. The milk that had dilute chocolate syrup added should not curdle.

Conclude and Apply
1. The common factor is that curdling occurred when acidic substances were added to the milk.
2. Answers will vary, but students should explain how their results supported or contradicted their hypotheses.

Going Further Cottage cheese is made by utilizing certain bacteria to acidify milk and produce curd. The curd is then separated from the whey, which is the remaining liquid portion. The curd might be heated and seasoned to produce cottage cheese. Making hard cheese is a more complicated process, and several variations of the process are used to make different types of cheeses. However, the first step in making any cheese is to extract curd from milk. After their research, students should appreciate the important role food science plays in meeting societies' needs.

Inquiry Activity 18.....................Page 35
Cabbage Chemistry

Purpose Students will learn about pH indicators and use a pH indicator (cabbage juice) to determine whether different solutions are acidic or basic.

Inquiry Skills Reinforced asking questions, designing an experiment, conducting an experiment, making observations, describing, analyzing data, forming conclusions, communicating

Time Required one class period

Background Red and purple cabbage; deep red leaves; red, purple, and blue flower petals and fruit contain pigments of the anthocyanin family. Anthocyanins release hydroxyl ions [OH^-] when placed in an acid and hydrogen ions [H^+] when placed in a base. In short, they react differently to acids and bases and can be used as acidity/basicity indicators.

Possible Procedure Students label their test tubes and add the same amount of cabbage juice, about 10 mL, to each one. To each test tube, they add the same amount, about 10 drops, of a different solution and stir. They record which test tube received which solution and the color of the mixture.

Preparation Tips
- To prepare the cabbage juice, cut a red or purple cabbage into small pieces. Place the cabbage pieces in a saucepan with enough water to cover and bring to a boil. Turn off the heat, stir, and let cool for 30 minutes. Strain the liquid into a jar, cover it, and refrigerate it until use. The juice will be purple, and most people will find the smell unpleasant. A liter of water cooked with half a cabbage will make about a liter of juice, enough for 25 students at 40 mL per student. Two liters of water and a whole cabbage should provide enough juice for spillage and extra experimenting. You can eat the cabbage later.
- The ammonia solution must be dilute because concentrated ammonia can produce dangerous fumes. To make a dilute solution, mix 1 part of household ammonia into 8 parts of distilled water.
- Other possible solutions might include lemon-lime soda, aspirin dissolved in water, and an antacid dissolved in water.
- Show students how to correctly read the bottom of the meniscus of the liquid in a graduated cylinder and how to use a stirring rod.
- Emphasize the importance of lab safety, especially wearing goggles and lab aprons and never directly smelling a sample. Long hair, sleeves, and bracelets require extra caution.

Interpret Your Data
1. Acids such as vinegar will turn the cabbage juice red; ammonia solution and baking soda (both bases) will turn the solution blue-green to green.
2. Independent variable: which solution was added; dependent variable: color change; constants include amount of solution used and temperature.

Conclude and Apply
1. The color change represents a sequence from the most acidic solution to the most basic solution.
2. Lemon juice is an acid. The color of the cabbage juice became more reddish.

Going Further The color progressively changes to purple (when the base neutralizes the acid) and then to a greenish color as the solution becomes basic. The base (ammonia solution) neutralized the acid (vinegar), and the cabbage juice indicator responded to the pH change by changing color.

States of Matter

Purpose Students will determine the temperature at which water freezes and boils. They also will learn that the temperature of water remains constant during a change of state.

Inquiry Skills Reinforced asking questions, forming hypotheses, designing an experiment, conducting an experiment, analyzing data, graphing, communicating

Time Required one period to perform the experiment and one period to make graphs and analyze data

Background During a change of state, the temperature of water remains constant. For example, when crushed ice first begins to melt, the temperature should be 0°C. The temperature of the ice/liquid water mixture will remain constant until all of the ice has melted. The heat energy that is added is used to change the state, so the temperature does not increase. Once all of the ice is melted, the temperature of the water begins to rise. The temperature also should remain constant at the boiling point (100°C). All of the heat added to water at the boiling point is used to convert liquid water to vapor.

Possible Procedure Students fill a beaker with crushed ice and place the beaker on a hot plate. They attach a thermometer clamp to a ring stand and put a Celsius thermometer in the clamp. The thermometer should hang down deeply into the crushed ice but should not touch the bottom of the beaker. Have the students take an initial reading. Caution them to allow the temperature recorded on the thermometer to stabilize. Students slowly heat the beaker and record data at regular intervals.

Preparation Tips
- The materials necessary for this activity can be purchased through laboratory supply catalogs.
- Crushed ice should be mostly free of salts because the salts are expelled during the freezing process. However, it is possible that the presence of dissolved solids in the water could cause the freezing and boiling points to differ slightly from the expected values. This problem can be avoided by making ice from distilled water.
- Atmospheric pressure will affect the boiling temperature of water. Water boils at 100°C at normal sea level pressure. If your location is at higher elevation, the boiling temperature will be lower than 100°C.
- To reduce the amount of materials needed, you might want to conduct the experiment as a class project.

Interpret Your Data
1. The last bit of ice should melt at about 0°C. The water should begin to boil at about 100°C. See *Preparation Tips* for possible complicating factors.
2. Students might need some help plotting their data and connecting data points. See *Conclude and Apply* for a description of the completed graph.

Conclude and Apply
1. Students' graphs should show the temperature of ice increasing to about 0°C, remaining constant as all ice is melted, liquid water temperature increasing to about 100°C at which boiling begins, and then the water temperature remaining constant at about 100°C.
2. Students might suggest molten metal solidifying into steel or butter melting on an ear of corn. An interesting example is dry ice changing directly to carbon dioxide gas, a process called sublimation.

Going Further Specific heat is defined as the amount of energy required to raise the temperature of 1 kg of a substance 1°C. Water is good for cooling machinery because it has a high specific heat. Tell students that water is good for cooling machinery because it can carry away a lot of heat without changing temperature too much.

Inquiry Activity 20......................Page 39
Isotopes and Atomic Mass

Purpose Students will learn how scientists derive the atomic masses of elements. They will become familiar with the terms *isotope* and *weighted average*.

Inquiry Skills Reinforced Asking questions, forming hypotheses, testing hypotheses, collecting data, analyzing data, making calculations, making models, communicating

Time Required One class period to develop a procedure, create models and tabulate data; *Interpret Your Data* and *Conclude and Apply* can be completed during that period or made into a separate lesson.

Background Students will need to be familiar with the concept of a percentage and how elements found in nature have certain percentages of each of their isotopes. As an example, ten grams of boron in the environment will contain about 8 grams of boron-11 and 2 grams of boron-10. One can show that "8 parts in 10" equals 8/10, or 80%.

You might want to explain the difference between a simple average and a weighted average to the students. For example, the simple average of the atomic masses of the isotopes of boron would be $(10+11)/2$, or 10.5; however, the weighted average of the isotopes would be $[(8 \times 11) + (2 \times 10)]/10$, or 10.8. One possible example to illustrate the concept of the weighted average is grade averaging: If an A is worth 4 points; a B, 3; a C, 2; a D, 1; and an F, 0, what will a student's grade average be if she has four As, two Bs, three Cs, no Ds, and one F? $[(4 \times 4) + (3 \times 2) + (2 \times 3) + (1 \times 0) + (0 \times 1)] / 10 = (16 + 6 + 6 + 0 + 0) / 10 = 28/10 = 2.8$.

Possible Procedure Students could be divided into teams of 2 or 3 to allow for group problem solving and possible division of responsibilities. Students will use cups to represent atoms and the two colors of beans to represent protons and neutrons. It is important to understand that each bean represents one atomic mass unit. An example of an appropriate model would be as follows:

For boron, students would have 8 cups containing 5 black beans (protons) and 6 white beans (neutrons), and 2 cups containing 5 black beans and 5 white beans. Therefore, in the table, they would have 2 atoms of mass number 10 and 8 atoms of mass number 11. The corresponding weighted average calculation for the atomic mass of boron would be, as above, $[(8 \times 11) + (2 \times 10)]/10$, or 10.8.

Preparation Tips Small paper cups and dry beans of different colors may be purchased at local grocery stores.

Interpret Your Data
1. The experimentally calculated atomic mass of boron should be 10.8.
2. The atomic mass listed on the periodic table is 10.811.

Conclude and Apply
1. One possible reason for the slight difference is that the percentage of the isotopes of this element was simplified for this experiment to allow a simple model to be made.
2. A possible response is the following: "Scientists find out the percent abundance of each isotope of an element that is found in nature, and use a weighted average of their atomic masses to determine the atomic mass of the element."

Going Further Radioactive tracers allow scientists to monitor the presence and concentration of an element or compound at a specific location. Highly radioactive isotopes would be inappropriate to use in human experiments.